Work Effectively in Finance

Tutorial

Michael Fardon

Published by Osborne Books Limited
Tel 01905 748071
Email books@osbornebooks.co.uk
Website www.osbornebooks.co.uk

Design by Laura Ingham

Printed by CPI Group (UK) Limited, Croydon, CRO 4YY, on environmentally friendly, acid-free paper from managed forests.

British Library Cataloguing in Publication Data
A catalogue record for this book is available from the British Library

ISBN 978 1909173 712

Contents

Also available from Osborne Books...

Workbooks

Practice questions and assessments
with answers

Wise Guides

Handy pocket-sized study and revision guides

Student Zone

Login to access your free ebooks and
interactive revision crosswords

Download **Osborne Books App** free from the App Store or Google Play Store
to view your ebooks online or offline on your mobile or tablet.

www.osbornebooks.co.uk

Introduction

Qualifications covered

This book has been written specifically to cover the Unit 'Work Effectively in Finance' which is mandatory for the following qualifications:

AAT Foundation Certificate in Accounting – Level 2

AAT Foundation Diploma in Accounting and Business – Level 2

AAT Foundation Certificate in Accounting at SCQF – Level 5

The book contains a clear text with worked examples and case studies, chapter summaries and key terms to help with revision. Each chapter concludes with a wide range of activities, many in the style of AAT computer based assessments.

Osborne Study and Revision Materials

Our materials are tailored to the needs of students studying this Unit and revising for the assessment. They include:

- **Workbooks:** paperback books with practice activities and exams
- **Wise Guides:** pocket-sized spiral bound revision cards
- **Student Zone:** access to Osborne Books online resources
- **Osborne Books App:** Osborne Books ebooks for mobiles and tablets

Visit www.osbornebooks.co.uk for details of study and revision resources and access to online material.

1 The finance function – roles and responsibilities

this chapter covers...

This chapter is an introduction to the role played by the finance function in an organisation such as a business. It describes the various areas in which finance staff are likely to work and how they provide information for other employees and also for people and organisations they deal with outside the business.

The chapter explains the following in detail:

■ *what is meant by 'finance' within a business*

■ *the difference between internal 'stakeholders' and external 'stakeholders'*

■ *the ways in which the finance function in an organisation provides information and support to both to other departments in the organisation and also to outside stakeholders*

■ *how basic accounting carried out by bookkeepers and accounts assistants involves a wide variety of areas – sales order processing, purchasing, cashiering, payroll, costing and stock control*

■ *the role of an accountant*

■ *reporting lines within the finance function*

■ *the ways in which the finance function within a business may include the production of statutory financial statements*

FINANCE FUNCTIONS

'finance' or 'accounting'?

This book is written to cover the requirements of a Certificate or Diploma in 'Accounting' and the Unit you are studying is 'Work Effectively in Finance'.

The two terms 'finance' and 'accounting' when applied to the context of a business organisation are very much interchangeable. The term 'finance function' will therefore normally be used within this text to refer to the department of an organisation that deals with financial transactions, accounting records, financial reports and costing.

the finance function and stakeholders

The finance function within an organisation is responsible to other people both within and outside the organisation. These people are known as **stakeholders**.

There are two main points to remember about 'stakeholders':

1   A stakeholder of an organisation (eg a business) is an individual, a group of people or an organisation that has **an interest or connection with the organisation** and is affected by what it does.

2   Stakeholders can be **external** to the organisation (eg customers, the Government) or **internal** (eg employees, other departments).

external stakeholders

Set out below are examples of **external stakeholders** of a business. In this case the business is a limited company.

-   **shareholders** – individual owners of a company who receive dividend payments paid out of profits made by the company; they may also have a role in managing the company

-   **banks** who lend money and provide other forms of finance; they will require financial projections of cash and profit to indicate whether or not repayments can be made

-   **customers** who depend on a business for good quality goods and services at a reasonable price and also for support of sustainability (eg supporting charity, the local community and energy saving)

-   **suppliers** who sell to a company, who want to see that it is financially sound and will regularly pay its bills

■ **regulatory bodies**, eg the UK Financial Reporting Council which requires that the company's accounts are properly prepared and accurately reported to stakeholders

■ **Government bodies** and **agencies** (eg HM Revenue & Customs [HMRC], which deals with the payment of tax and VAT returns)

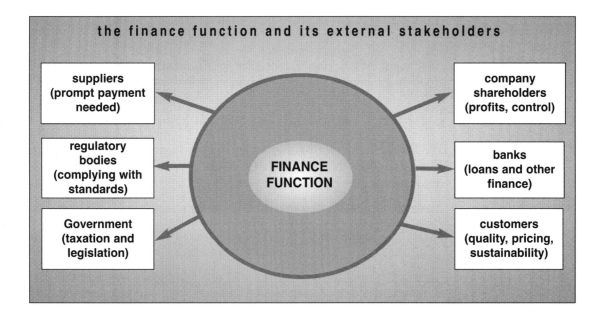

the finance function – internal support

Whatever the size of the business the finance function will carry out a variety of tasks to help keep the business running. In this case the finance function will treat the people or departments it is supporting as **internal stakeholders** because those people or departments rely on the finance function for support. Without the involvement of the finance department the business would not be able to continue operating.

The main operating areas of the finance function are as follows:

■ **sales order processing** – taking sales orders, producing invoices, monitoring receipts – all the jobs connected with the sales ledger

■ **purchasing** – sending out orders, checking the incoming documentation, making payments – all the jobs connected with the purchases ledger

■ **cashiering** – recording incoming and outgoing payments and dealing with cash held in the business – all the jobs connected with the cash book or the petty cash book

■ **payroll** – maintaining payroll records, calculating the payroll and processing payroll payments

Other specialist finance jobs include:

■ **costing** – working out the figures for the cost of products and services and preparing reports for management

■ **inventory control** – monitoring and re-ordering inventory

In the diagram below the white boxes show the individual areas of the finance function and the remaining text shows how they support the various departments of the business.

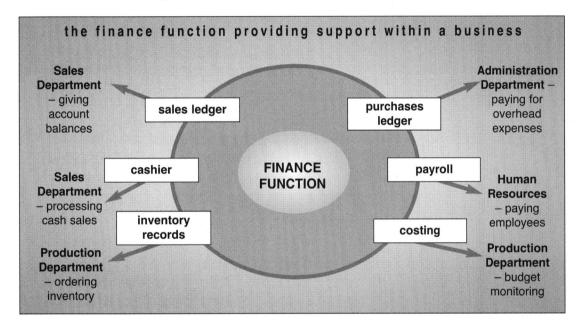

the finance function providing support within a business

- Sales Department – giving account balances
- Sales Department – processing cash sales
- Production Department – ordering inventory
- sales ledger
- cashier
- inventory records
- **FINANCE FUNCTION**
- purchases ledger
- payroll
- costing
- Administration Department – paying for overhead expenses
- Human Resources – paying employees
- Production Department – budget monitoring

examples of information provided by the finance function

■ the sales ledger section can keep sales representatives updated with the credit status of their customers, highlighting any slow payers

■ the purchases ledger section can advise the Administration Department of how much is owed to suppliers for purchases and overhead expenses

■ the payroll section can advise the Human Resources Department about payroll costs, for example how much overtime was paid last month

■ the costing section can advise the Production Department on the direct costs of production (eg materials) and also the overhead costs of production

■ the cashier handles and records the cash sales for the Sales Department and provides cash for a petty cash system

THE ROLE OF AN ACCOUNTANT

the accountant

In larger organisations, accountants form the next level up from the accounts assistants. They include:

- **financial accountants**
- **management accountants**
- **auditors**

financial accountant

The function of the **financial accountant** is concerned with financial transactions, and using the information produced by the bookkeeper or accounts assistant. The financial accountant extracts information from the accounting records in order to provide a method of control, for example, over customers who buy on credit, over suppliers, cash and bank balances. The role of a financial accountant also involves the analysis and reporting of financial data so that financial statements – for example, the Statement of Profit or Loss – can be prepared for internal use and also for external use.

management accountant

The **management accountant** obtains information about costs – eg the cost of labour, materials, expenses (overheads) – and interprets the data and prepares reports and budgets for the owners or managers of the business. The management accountant is concerned with financial decision-making, planning and control of the business.

auditors

Auditors are accountants whose role is to check that accounting procedures have been followed correctly. There are two types of auditors: **external auditors** and **internal auditors**.

External auditors are independent of the business whose accounts are being audited. They are normally members of firms of accountants. The most common type of audit conducted by external auditors is the audit of larger limited companies. This is a legal requirement.

Internal auditors are employed or contracted by the business which they audit. Their duties are concerned with the internal check and control procedures of the business, for example monitoring the procedures for the control of cash, and the authorisation of purchases.

REPORTING LINES

the structure of the business

The top diagram on the next page is based on the finance roles in a company. The boxes with the dark grey background all represent finance roles. You will see that the structure is set out in a series of layers of authority and responsibility. This type of structure is known as a '**hierarchy**' – the lowest level includes the bookkeepers and accounts assistants, and as you move up the structure, the people involved gain both power and responsibility.

The bottom diagram on the next page shows the structure of a small accountancy practice. The same principle of levels of hierarchy applies in this case.

reporting lines between levels

You will also see that the arrows in both the diagrams represent 'up and down' **reporting lines** within the organisation. A reporting line means that the people lower down in the structure always report to the next layer up. In the case of the company, accounts assistants report to line managers, who in turn report to the senior managers, who in turn report to the directors. The same principle of reporting lines applies to the accounting practice.

Note that the word 'report' here has various meanings. For example, a lower level is able to pass on to a higher level:

■ specific information that is required or has been requested

■ regular reports that are needed

■ day-to-day work for approval and authorisation

■ complaints about the work, work conditions or colleagues

■ suggestions about how to improve the way the work is organised

It follows that the higher level in the company has the authority to:

■ request information

■ commission reports

■ approve and authorise work carried out at the lower level

■ deal with complaints and resolve the issue (or pass it to the next level up)

■ organise discussions about the way the work is organised

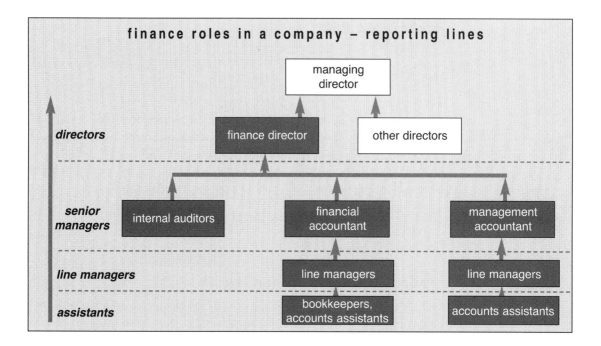

finance roles in a company – reporting lines

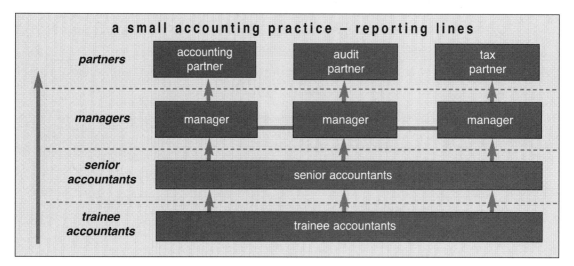

a small accounting practice – reporting lines

other reporting lines

In addition to the formal 'up and down' reporting lines described above there are other identifiable reporting lines within an organisation. These include:

■ people **on the same level** of authority, possibly working in a different section of the same department and regularly providing information and reports, for example, a payroll assistant providing details to the cashier of cash required for the weekly cash wage packets

■ people **on a different level** of authority and reported to for a specific function within the organisation, for example an accounts assistant

- reporting to a training manager to have a talk about training needs

- reporting as a representative of the finance department elected to the company social committee to arrange the next night out on the town

the need for effective working

If an organisation is to work effectively, smoothly and without any hitches, it is important that the reporting lines operate efficiently. This means that the management of the organisation must ensure, for example, that:

■ finance tasks must be carefully checked by a more senior person – eg the issue of a sales invoice, the preparation of payroll

■ finance tasks must be authorised – eg the approval for payment of a purchase invoice, processing of payroll

■ problems with any accounting system should be reported to a higher authority

■ requests for information or a report should be clear and a realistic timescale indicated

The same holds true for reporting lines which involve people on the same level or people such as training managers. It is critical that all employees should know:

■ the identity and status of the people to whom they should report

■ what they have to report

If this is not made clear to employees there will be communication problems with the reporting lines, errors are likely to be made and complaints will be received. This could result in money losses and damage to the reputation of the organisation. As mentioned earlier, in a small business the finance tasks are likely to be carried out by a limited number of people. In this case there will not be many reporting lines but the need for efficiency by the few people involved will become all the more important.

STATUTORY FINANCIAL STATEMENTS

what are the statutory statements?

The finance function of a limited company will be responsible for producing the data for any **statutory financial statements** produced by the company. There are three main statements which will be produced to report to the management and the shareholders the financial activity and performance of a company during its most recent financial year. These three statements are:

■ The **Statement of Profit or Loss** (also known as the Profit and Loss Account) which is calculated as:

income minus expenses = profit (or loss)

This shows the level of profitability of a company (or any loss).

■ The **Statement of Financial Position** (also known as the Balance Sheet) which is calculated as:

assets minus liabilities = capital

You may already be familiar with this in your study of the 'accounting equation' in the Bookkeeping Transactions Unit. The **Statement of Financial Position** is an indicator of the financial strength of the business, showing how much it owns and how it is financed.

■ The **Statement of Cash Flows** shows the amount of money flowing in and out of a limited company during the financial year. It is based on figures drawn from the Statement of Profit or Loss and the Statement of Financial Position. Its main purpose is to highlight how much cash the business has at the end of the year, where it has come from and whether it has increased or decreased. In basic terms it states:

cash at the beginning of the year plus increase in cash during the year (or minus decrease in cash during the year) = cash at the end of the year

It is often said that 'Cash is King' – and this is very true in relation to a business where a shortage of cash can cause a business to fail.

who has to draw up the statutory statements?

It is important to note that many businesses will not have to draw up all these documents. The statutory statements will only have to be drawn up and sent to Companies House by the largest companies. Smaller companies (including micro-entities) are normally only required to draw up 'abbreviated accounts' the extent of which will depend on the size of the company. The statements will then be made publicly available for anyone to inspect. There may well be interested parties who will want to see how financially sound a company is, for example investors in the company and any bank providing it with finance.

These statements will normally be drawn up by the external accountants who have audited the company's accounts and will have the figures available.

management accounts and the finance function

The three statements described above may be drawn up by the finance function of a business to be used as 'management accounts' for internal managers who need to see how the business is getting on in terms of sales, profitability, the amount of borrowing and the cash position.

Chapter Summary

■ The **finance function** is a term which describes the work carried out by the finance department of an organisation such as a business.

■ A **stakeholder** is a group of people or an organisation that has an interest or connection with the organisation and is affected by what it does.

■ The finance function deals with **external stakeholders** such as the shareholders of a company, banks, customers, suppliers, Government and regulatory bodies.

■ The finance function deals with **internal stakeholders** by supplying support to other people and departments within the business.

■ The main operating areas of the finance function include:
- sales order processing
- purchasing
- cashiering
- payroll
- costing
- inventory control

■ **Accountants** have responsibility for various areas of the finance function, including the recording of financial information, financial reporting, forecasting, planning and managing.

■ **Financial accountants** deal with the reporting of past financial transactions and their presentation in financial statements for internal and external use.

■ **Management accountants** provide past and projected financial data to managers so that forward planning can take place in the form of budgets, and decisions made about the use of resources.

■ **Auditors** are accountants whose role it is to check that accounting procedures have been followed correctly. Internal auditors are employees of the organisation and look over its accounting systems; external auditors are independent firms of accountants who verify the accounts.

■ A **reporting line** is the direct relationship between a manager and the people who work under him/her. It involves the passing of information, suggestions and complaints. Well-developed reporting lines are essential in any well-run organisation, especially the larger organisations.

■ The finance function is responsible for providing **statutory financial statements** if required by Companies House. These include the Statement of Profit or Loss, the Statement of Financial Position and the Statement of Cash Flows.

Key Terms		
	finance function	the department of an organisation such as a business that deals with financial transactions, accounting records, financial reports and costing
	stakeholder	a person, group of people or organisation that has an interest in the performance of an organisation such as a business
	internal stakeholder	a section of a business which relies on another part of the business for information and support
	external stakeholder	a person, group of people or organisation outside a business that has an interest in its performance
	reporting line	the line of communication between different levels within an organisation
	accounting	the process of recording, analysing and reporting financial information
	financial accounting	the analysis and reporting of past financial transactions in financial reports
	management accounting	providing past and projected financial information for managers to help with planning, decision making and control
	internal auditing	internal checking of the financial records by an employee of the organisation
	external auditing	external checking of the financial records by independent accountants
	statutory financial statements	a financial report which is required by law to be sent to Companies House by the larger limited companies

Activities

1.1 The most appropriate description of the 'finance function' in an organisation such as a business is:

(a)	It is limited to cash handling and the raising of finance	
(b)	It is limited to financial records and financial reports	
(c)	It deals with financial records, financial reports and customer marketing	
(d)	It deals with cash, financial records, financial reports, costing and budgets	

Tick the **one** correct option.

1.2 Indicate with a tick which of the following would be considered an external stakeholder of a limited company business:

(a)	HM Revenue & Customs	
(b)	The board of directors of the company	
(c)	The company's bank	
(d)	The customers of the business	
(e)	The employees of the business	
(f)	The suppliers of the business	

1.3 A financial accountant is a person who

(a)	Prepares sales and profit reports for senior management	
(b)	Sets budgets for the next financial year	
(c)	Checks the accounting procedures used within a business	

Tick the **one** correct option.

1.4 A management accountant is a person who

(a)	Prepares a Statement of Profit or Loss for the last financial year	
(b)	Manages the payroll function of a business	
(c)	Interprets costing data for senior management	

Tick the **one** correct option.

1.5 Complete the following sentence by using the correct terms set out in bold print below.

external auditor   internal auditor

An [   ] is normally an employee of the organisation being audited, but an [   ] should be a member of an independent firm of accountants.

1.6 The following sentences relate to the statutory financial statements drawn up by a limited company and submitted to Companies House. Indicate in the appropriate column whether they are true or false.

		True	**False**
(a)	They are drawn up by all limited companies, small or large		
(b)	They set out the company's financial position for next year		
(c)	They are only required for larger limited companies		
(d)	They include reports on last year's profit and cash position		

1.7   The diagram below shows the organisational structure of an accounts department in a small business which buys and sells goods on credit.

Study the diagram and answer the questions that follow.

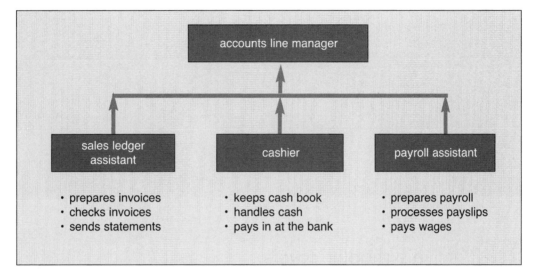

(a)   Identify the three reporting lines in the diagram.

(b)   Which assistant would the line manager ask if she wanted a report on customers who were bad payers?

(c)   If the payroll assistant wanted to complain that there was not the right number of £20 notes collected from the bank for the wage packets, to whom would he complain

   (1)   in the first place?

   (2)   in the second place, if there was still a problem?

(d)   What other 'assistant level' accounting roles might also feature in this diagram, which shows a business that buys and sells goods on credit?

2 Effective working in the finance function

this chapter covers...

This chapter examines the way in which the finance function of a business should be run so that the organisation operates effectively and presents a positive picture to other businesses and customers.

This requires that the finance function of a business should:

■ *encourage good working relationships between its staff and with other departments*

■ *establish good working relationship with other businesses*

■ *communicate well within the business and also externally; this means that any communication should be clearly expressed, complete, accurate and on time*

■ *ensure that working practices are efficient within the finance function*

■ *ensure that the business remains solvent, ie that it can pay its debts when they need to be paid*

■ *comply with operational policies and procedures for the finance function, for example dealing with cash, ordering supplies, making payments*

■ *comply with policies and procedures for the whole organisation, for example the use of mobile phones and the requirements of Health & Safety*

WORKING EFFECTIVELY – GOOD BUSINESS RELATIONSHIPS

the meaning of 'effective' working

The word 'effective', which is used in the name of the Unit – 'Work Effectively in Finance' – means:

being successful in achieving what you set out to do

For a finance function in an organisation such as a business to be successful and 'effective' it needs to establish good working relationships:

- **internally** – with members of the finance 'team' and also with other functions of the business, ie other departments such as Sales, Marketing, Administration

- **externally** – with customers and other external stakeholders

internal business relationships

It is important for any team such as a finance function to achieve its goals by respecting and building positive relations with work colleagues:

- in the **finance function**; this involves

  - complying with the requests of managers promptly

  - complying with the requests of other work colleagues

  - working according to defined work procedures

  - helping out work colleagues when you think help is needed, for example if they are stressed out with too much work or if they are new to the job and need guidance and reassurance

- carrying out requests for information from **other functions** (departments) in the business, for example:

  - complying with the requests of managers from other departments, eg financial spreadsheets needed for a meeting

  - providing regular information to other functions, eg sales figures to the Sales function

If members of the finance function are not prepared to comply with these types of request promptly and positively both the finance function and the whole business can be affected in a negative way. This will have consequences not only for the finance function but also the whole business, its relations with is stakeholders, and particularly with its customers.

external business relationships

It is equally important for the finance function to ensure that it promotes a good working relationship with its customers and other external stakeholders:

■ customers like to be treated promptly, with courtesy and provided with information that is accurate

■ this will give the business a good reputation which means that the customer is likely to recommend it to other potential customers

■ if the customers of a business are happy it means that the staff who deal with the customers are also likely to be happy and motivated

■ a happy customer is also a loyal customer and a loyal customer helps to maintain the sales income and ultimately the profit of the business

COMMUNICATION AND EFFECTIVE WORKING

If you are communicating a message to another person or group of people, that message must be **effective** to be successful. It must achieve its aim and be:

■ clear and easily understood

■ concise – not too long-winded

■ unambiguous, ie using straightforward language so that the meaning cannot be misinterpreted

■ complete – the whole message must be there

■ accurate – there is no point in unintentionally misleading people

■ provided at the right time – not too early and not too late

■ appropriate to the person or people receiving it

■ in the most appropriate format, whether by phone, text, email or letter

On a personal level, if you are organising a meal out with a group of friends, you will need to email, phone or text instructions giving clear details of the place, date and time and asking for confirmation.

You need to provide all this information in good time to the right people and be available to receive replies. You need to make sure the instructions are very clear otherwise the meal could turn out to be a non-event.

This is a very basic comparison, but the same principles apply to any workplace situation.

workplace communication – the people involved

Communication can be very varied. If you think about a working day and compile a list of all the forms of communication you get involved in you would find that you would be recording:

■ **internal communications** – with colleagues, line managers and anyone else involved in your reporting lines

■ **external communications** – depending on your role in the organisation, this could be with customers, suppliers, the bank, carriers and the local sandwich or pizza delivery company

If you are communicating **within the organisation** you should

■ choose the most appropriate method

■ be polite – even if you do not feel like it at the time

■ act promptly – do not leave things to later, they may never happen

If you are communicating **with outsiders** you should

■ choose the most appropriate method of communication

■ communicate clearly, accurately and promptly

■ present a professional approach

■ comply with 'corporate image' – this may mean using standard letters and forms, or speaking on the telephone using standard 'scripts'

The need to develop effective communication skills will be covered in full in Chapter 4 of this book.

AN EFFICIENT ORGANISATION

the need for efficiency

The last chapter explained how the finance function of an organisation should support the other departments by providing information. As we have already seen it is critical that this information is:

■ **complete** – all the information needed is provided

■ **accurate** – the information must be 100% correct

■ **on time** – the information should be provided within the given timescale

If all these three conditions listed above are fulfilled by the staff working in accounting and finance roles, it contributes to the **efficiency** of the organisation – its smooth running and its profitability.

'Efficiency' can be described as:

'achieving the right result with the minimum of wasted time, effort or expense.'

Efficiency is an important objective for any organisation.

achieving efficiency in the workplace

There are various ways in which efficiency in the workplace can be maintained and improved:

- by the **individual employee**:

    – treating other employees and management with respect

    – taking pride in the tasks performed and making sure that the accounting procedures are fully understood

    – being familiar with and updating when necessary the various accounting tasks in written form (a 'procedures manual') for the benefit of others who are training on the job (see pages 23-24)

    – pursuing CPD 'Continuing Professional Development' - ie training and qualifications for the job (see Chapter 7)

- by the **employer**:

    – treating the employees with respect and encouraging motivation

    – ensuring that accounting procedures are followed properly

    – arranging appropriate training (as part of CPD) so that each employee's job is done properly and expertly

    – ensuring that there is sufficient staff to cover the required finance tasks

    – making sure the staff do not work very long hours and are paid an acceptable wage

THE NEED FOR SOLVENCY

'Solvency' means being able to pay your debts when they are due.

You are 'solvent' when you can pay your debts and 'insolvent 'when you cannot.

For a business organisation – for example a chain of shops, a bank or a football club – the inability to pay debts when they are due means that the business has become **insolvent**. This can result in court action, closure of the business and the loss of jobs. It also means that suppliers who are owed money are likely to lose most or all of what they are owed.

How does all this relate to the efficiency of the finance function of an organisation such as a business? A business needs to know that it will have enough money in the bank to be able to pay its debts. This means that the finance function will have to provide accurate and complete information to management about:

■ how much money it has **at present**

■ how much money it will have coming in and going out **in the future**

Specifically it will need to know accurate details of:

money in:

■ the balance of money in the bank account

■ amounts coming in from customers and when they are due

money out:

■ amounts due to suppliers and for other expenses and when they are due

All this will be calculated by the business in a forecast known as a **cash budget**, which you will need to draw up in your later studies. It is important that the information provided by the various sections of the accounting and finance function must be accurate and complete, and provided on time.

the need for working capital and being solvent

The surplus of:

■ money in, money due and money that can be quickly realised . . . over

■ money due to be paid out

is known as **working capital**.

As long as 'money in, money due in and money realisable' is greater than 'money to be paid out', working capital is positive and the business **can pay its debts when they are due**, ie it is **solvent**.

Careful management of working capital by the finance function is very important if the business is to remain solvent. There are some basic rules to observe:

■ pay money (cash and cheques) into the bank account as soon as possible; do not leave it for a long time in the office before processing it

■ negotiate 'long' credit periods with your suppliers - ie pay them as late as you can without breaching any agreements, eg after 60 days

■ make sure your credit customers pay up on time and try and keep the payment terms as 'short' as possible, ie 30 days rather than 90 days

So, if you pay in at the bank at least once a week, offer 30 days terms to your customers and pay your suppliers after 60 days you are making efficient use of your resources and should have enough working capital to keep you trading.

But problems can arise when there is less money coming in than going out. A new business can sometimes run into trouble, for example, if does not manage its working capital efficiently, as the following Case Study shows.

Case Study

JIMMY CASH: WORKING CAPITAL AND SOLVENCY

situation

Jimmy Cash has recently started business importing home alarm systems. He has put £25,000 of his savings into the bank and negotiated with four main suppliers who have asked for payment of their invoices within 30 days.

Jimmy has been phoning around to sell his products to shops and mail order firms. He is pleased with the response, although a number of his customers have asked for payment terms of 60 days, saying that 'You will have to give me 60 days if you want the business'.

Sales for the first three months go well and Jimmy has taken on two new employees to deal with the volume of orders received. Things have been so busy in this period that Jimmy has been unable to get to the bank very often to pay in the cheques that have started to arrive. He has also received calls from two of his suppliers chasing payment of their invoices and threatening cutting off supplies if he does not pay up. He is also aware that some of his customers have not settled their first invoices.

At the end of the three months he gets a call from the bank asking him to call in to discuss his bank account which is now £5,000 overdrawn.

Jimmy asks for your help and advice.

solution

You tell Jimmy that he is in a dangerous situation because he has not managed his working capital properly and may be insolvent, ie he may not be able to settle his debts (to the bank and his suppliers) from the money coming in from his sales to customers.

You advise Jimmy

- to request the bank to allow him to pay off the overdraft over the next six months
- to chase up any customers who are late paying and to bank their cheques
- to try and negotiate a longer payment period from his suppliers

Jimmy has basically ignored the need for careful cash management, and despite running a successful business, is in immediate danger of becoming insolvent.

Note: this important principle of cash management is also covered in Chapter 2 of the Osborne Books tutorial text 'Bookkeeping Controls'.

ORGANISATIONAL POLICIES AND PROCEDURES

The next section of this chapter deals with the **policies and procedures** set down by an organisation for dealing with a variety of areas, including the finance function.

These regulations are often set down in a series of manuals which should be updated regularly and readily available for reference by employees. You need to know that some of the principles set out in these manuals will be established in law, but you will not need to know details of the laws. An extract from a Policies and Procedures document for the finance function is set out on the next page.

We will first describe the **policies and procedures** which affect the accounting processes which are carried out in the finance function.

maintaining accounting records – companies

The law relating to limited companies (Companies Act) requires that companies should keep the following accounting records:

- records of entries made of payments received and made by the company and a description of each entry
- a record of the assets (items owned) and liabilities (items owed)
- records of inventory held

These records include financial documents and books of account such as purchase orders, invoices, credit notes, daybooks, cash book, petty cash book and, importantly, a full set of ledger accounts.

This is a description of a fairly standard system of accounting records. An important objective of any company is that this system should be accurate, complete and up-to-date.

accounting records – other organisations

The principles that apply to the accounting records of companies are also applied to other business organisations.

Accounting records, whether paper-based or on computer, should be:

- complete
- accurate
- up-to-date
- accessible – so that information can be extracted for the owners and managers (a need illustrated in the Case Study on the previous page)

POLICIES AND PROCEDURES STATEMENT (extract)

Books of account and records
Proper accounting records will be kept. The accounts systems is based around computer facilities, using Sage and Excel, but manual/paper records will also be used if appropriate. The following records will be kept:

- Appropriate control accounts (bank control, petty cash control, VAT control, salary control)
- Monthly trial balances
- Petty cash and bank accounts will be reconciled at least monthly
- VAT returns produced on the required quarterly cycle

Ordering supplies and services
Budget holders can place orders for goods or services within their budget areas, subject only to cash-flow restraints. All orders of £1,000 or more must be authorised by the budget holder, except for specific areas of expenditure where written procedures have been agreed. Under £1,000, the budget holder may delegate all ordering as appropriate. Budget holders will discuss with the Financial Controller appropriate parameters, plus maximum allowed deviations before the budget holder or senior manager is brought in, which will be documented.

Payment authorisation and Purchases Ledger
All invoices must be authorised for payment by the budget holder, although the actual checking of details may be delegated. The authorising department is responsible for checking invoices for accuracy in terms of figures and conformity with the order placed, that the services or goods have been received, and following up any problems. Finance must be informed if there are queries delaying authorisation or if payment is to be withheld for any reason.

A Purchases Ledger is operated by Finance. All incoming invoices are to be passed to Finance section as soon as they arrive. Invoices will be recorded in the Purchases Ledger within two days, unless there are coding problems. They are then passed on to budget holders for authorisation. Once authorised as above, suppliers will be paid within the appropriate timescale.

Cheque writing and signing
Signatories will only be drawn from senior staff and directors, and any new signatory must be approved by the directors before the bank is notified. All cheques for £1,000 or over require two signatories. Cheque signatories should check that the expenditure has been authorised by the appropriate person before signing the cheque. Salary payments require the signature of the Accounts Manager or Financial Controller, plus one other. Cheques should be filled in completely (with payee, amount in words and figures, and date) before cheques are signed.

Handling of cash
Petty cash will be topped up on the 'imprest' system, where the amount spent is reimbursed. It is intended for small items, up to £20. Anything over this should be paid by cheque where possible. The imprest has a balance limit of £250. The petty cash balance will be reconciled when re-storing the imprest balance, or monthly if this is more frequent. All cash collected from Finance will be signed for, and receipts will be issued for all cash returned.

reporting lines and authorisation

As mentioned in the last chapter, **reporting lines** are an important element in an accounting system. Each employee is placed within a certain level of authority and will report to a higher level which will be given the responsibility of **authorising** whatever it is that the more junior employee is required to do. Typical transactions and documents which require authorisation include:

■ authorisation of purchases (the signing of purchase orders)

■ the making of payments (signing cheques, BACS payment orders)

■ paying in at the bank (signing the paying in slip)

■ petty cash payments (signing the petty cash voucher)

■ payroll processing (checking and signing the payment instructions)

If the organisation is a large one the authorisation process may be more complex. For example:

■ authorising payments (including the signing of cheques) up to £1,000 may require one signature, whereas payments of £1,000 or more may require two signatures

■ authorisation of payroll payments may require a senior manager's signature

If, however, it is a small business organisation with only five employees, there will be far fewer regulations of this type. It may be that the 'boss' will authorise everything and will delegate this when he or she goes on holiday.

The important point of all this is that employees should:

■ know what needs authorising and by whom

■ keep to the regulations with no short-cuts being taken

The organisation will then run far more efficiently and smoothly. If there are any problems or errors, the person responsible can be identified and the problem resolved and the errors corrected.

retention of accounting records

Another requirement for the smooth running of an organisation is that its accounting records should be retained in accessible form in case of future queries, or even future legal action against the organisation.

Businesses normally have a retention policy stating that records are kept for six years, plus the current year. The reasons for this are based on law. Tax and company law generally require records to be kept for at least six years.

maintaining payroll records

Payroll records are very sensitive because they involve the rates of pay of all the employees of an organisation. They have to be maintained:

- accurately – because they involve personal pay
- securely – to avoid fraud taking place
- confidentially – because of their sensitive nature

More often than not payroll records are kept on computer. Organisations should regulate access to this electronic data very strictly, normally through the use of passwords issued only to authorised personnel.

It is essential that all payroll records – whether paper-based or computerised – are complete, accurate and up-to-date at all times.

maintaining VAT records

HM Revenue & Customs (HMRC) regulates the UK indirect tax **Value Added Tax** (VAT) which is charged on sales of goods and services and paid regularly by the organisation to the government.

It is very important that the accounting records and financial documents which involve VAT are complete and in order. Any calculations using the VAT rate must use the correct percentage for the appropriate date, as the government has a habit of changing the VAT rate from time to time.

The accounting records and financial documents involved include:

- invoices
- credit notes
- receipts
- petty cash vouchers
- day books
- the cash book and the petty cash book
- the VAT account in the double-entry bookkeeping system

As noted above, it is critical that these records and documents are accurately completed and checked by the accounting staff as a matter of daily routine.

OFFICE MANAGEMENT POLICIES AND PROCEDURES

An efficient organisation will have well-established and documented policies and procedures covering a wide range of issues relating to staff behaviour and office organisation. These are documented in manuals which should be read by all staff in all areas of the business. These include:

- a **code of conduct** – covering issues such as the use of the internet and emails, mobile phones, drug and alcohol policy
- **health and safety** – maintaining a safe and hazard-free working environment
- **confidentiality** – ensuring security of customer data
- **'green' policies** – saving the planet through conservation of energy and recycling

Confidentiality is dealt with in detail in the next chapter and **green' policies** are covered in Chapter 8 which explains 'Sustainability' issues.

a code of conduct

A code of conduct will define acceptable and unacceptable staff behaviour. An efficient office will not tolerate behaviour which will disrupt the normal work flow, as in the following two cases:

> No employee is to start work, or return to work while under the influence of alcohol or drugs. A breach of this policy is grounds for disciplinary action, up to and including termination of employment.
>
> Using the organisation's computer resources to seek out, access or send any material of an offensive, obscene or defamatory nature is prohibited and may result in disciplinary action.

Harsh rules, however, do not always increase efficiency. Some employers allow the personal use of the internet or mobile phones in employees' free time at work and find that this improves employees' work rate and efficiency.

health and safety at work

Responsibility for health and safety in the workplace lies both with the **employee** and the **employer**. You should be aware that there are many different laws governing this area, the most well-known of which is the **Health and Safety at Work Act**. You do not need to know these laws but you should be aware of the principles which they establish. Their aims are:

- to ensure that health and safety measures are introduced and observed both by employers and employees
- to specify the rights and responsibilities of employers and employees
- to enable employees to obtain compensation in the case of injury or ill health caused by conditions in the workplace

The law requires that every employer that employs five or more employees must draw up a written **Health and Safety Policy Statement**. This document (see below) often takes the form of a loose-leaf manual which can be updated from time to time. The Statement must be shown to every employee. Employers then obtain each employee's signature on a form saying that they have read it.

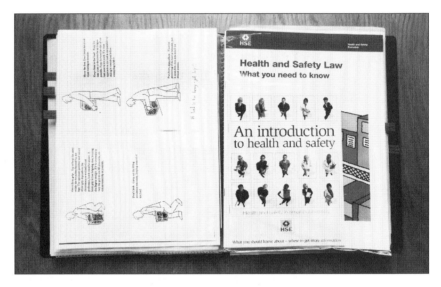

The Health and Safety Policy Statement is likely to contain:

- the names of the people responsible for health and safety
- the need for safety when employees operate machinery, handle unsafe substances or lift heavy objects (see left hand page in the picture above)
- the need and procedures for employees to report accidents, serious illnesses or fatalities in the workplace
- the forms needed (including copies) for reporting accidents and hazards

If the finance function is to be efficient and well run it should therefore avoid:

- electrical hazards – trailing leads and cables
- blockages and obstacles to progress – filing drawers left open, waste bins in the way, boxes stacked up in corridors
- fire doors wedged open (ie safety doors that normally swing shut)
- employees taking unnecessary risks – standing on chairs and desks, lifting items that are too heavy or not bending properly when lifting
- using a computer workstation and not taking regular breaks or not using suitable seating

■ **Effective working** in an organisation means the organisation is successful in what it sets out to do.

■ An important aspect of effective working in the finance function of a business means being successful in establishing **good working relationships**. These relationships should not only be with customers and other external stakeholders but also internally within the finance function and with other departments.

■ **Efficiency** in an organisation means achieving the right result with the minimum of wasted time, effort or expense. Efficiency is an important objective of effective working.

■ **Communication** within an organisation and with outsiders must be effective to be successful. This means it must be clear, concise, accurate and delivered on time. It must also be in the most appropriate format.

■ **Solvency** means being able to pay debts when they are due. If there is a shortage of cash there is a risk of insolvency. The finance function must monitor and control the cash position to prevent the cash from running out.

■ **Policies and procedures** are internal documents which regulate a wide variety of areas of the business. Each function, eg the finance function, will have its own policies and procedures, eg for the authorisation of purchases, payments, cheques and details of who can sign different types of authorisation.

■ The finance function will be subject to **external regulations**, some of them set down in law, which must be complied with, for example payroll, VAT and Health & Safety.

effective working	being successful in what you set out to do
efficiency	achieving the right result with the minimum of wasted time, effort or expense
solvency	being able to repay your debts when they are due
policies and procedures	regulations set down by an organisation for the running of defined areas of activity, eg payroll
health and safety	the aspects of an organisation which involve both employer and employee having regard for a healthy and safe working environment for all concerned

Activities

2.1 The meaning of 'effective working' is as follows. Tick the correct option.

(a)	Being successful in achieving what you set out to do	
(b)	Completing what you have to do as soon as possible	
(c)	Creating the maximum effect in order to improve performance	
(d)	Always complying with the requests of colleagues	

2.2 Which **one** of the following is the most accurate definition of efficiency? Tick the correct option.

(a)	To complete a job as quickly as possible at all costs	
(b)	To complete a job with the minimum of wasted time, effort or expense	
(c)	To complete a job exactly as described in the Policies and Procedures	
(d)	To complete a job using the cheapest way of doing it	

2.3 Which **two** of the following are qualities of an effective communication? Tick the correct options.

(a)	It needs to be made as quickly as possible	
(b)	It must be made within an appropriate timescale	
(c)	It needs to be made using language appropriate to the situation	
(d)	It needs to be made using formal and complex business language	

2.4 A customer sends your business a rude email containing inappropriate words, complaining about poor customer service. What should you do? Tick the most appropriate response.

(a)	Ignore the email completely because the customer is so rude	
(b)	Reply using similar language	
(c)	Reply politely with apologies	
(d)	Reply and tell the customer that it is unacceptable to use bad language	

2.5   The policies and procedures for the finance function are likely to include:

(a)	Details of the authorisation needed for business purchases	
(b)	Details of annual appraisals of finance staff	
(c)	Records of customer names and addresses	
(d)	Passwords for all the computers in the business	

Which **one** of these is correct? Tick the correct option.

2.6   Which of the following is the most accurate definition of solvency of a business?

(a)	Receiving all customer payments on the due date	
(b)	Having a lot of money in the bank	
(c)	Being able to pay all company debts when they are due	
(d)	Delaying paying money into the bank as soon as it is received	

Tick the **one** correct option.

2.7   If a business wants to improve its working capital position it should:

(a)	Pay suppliers earlier	
(b)	Get customers to pay earlier	
(c)	Pay employees' wages earlier	
(d)	Pay in at the bank less frequently	

Tick the **one** correct option.

2.8   A Health and Safety Policy Statement is:

(a)	Issued each year by the Government to help protect employees at work	
(b)	Drawn up by employees to state their rights to personalise their working area	
(c)	A list of the accidents and fatalities at work each year	
(d)	Drawn up by the employer as a guide to employees of health and safety arrangements	

Tick the **one** correct option.

3 Financial information, documentation and data security

this chapter covers...

People working within the finance function will deal on a day-to-day basis with a wide range of financial information and documents. In order to work effectively they must be familiar with the types of information and documents involved. These include:

■ *Information and documents received from external stakeholders, for example:*
  - *from customers: purchase orders, remittance advices*
  - *from suppliers: quotations, invoices, credit notes, statements of account*
  - *statements from the bank and credit card company*

■ *Other information and documents internally produced by the finance function for management, who need to monitor the financial performance of the business and make appropriate financial decisions:*
  - *sales figures and costs for budgeting purposes*
  - *the cash position of the business*
  - *financial statements to show profitability and borrowing made*
  - *the tax that is likely to have to be paid*

■ *The finance function will only run smoothly and efficiently if the information given and documents prepared are complete, accurate and produced on time.*

■ *People working in the finance function must appreciate that the information, documents and data they use must be stored safely and securely. This will be made possible by:*
  - *restricting access by using suitable passwords*
  - *ensuring that all financial data and documents are regularly backed up or stored*

FINANCIAL DOCUMENTS RECEIVED

documents received from a purchaser

If you are studying the AAT Certificate or Diploma in Accounting Unit 'Bookkeeping Transactions' you will already be familiar with the various documents that pass between buyer and seller. The two documents illustrated below – the purchase order and remittance advice – will be received from the purchaser. The finance staff of the seller must have a good working knowledge of both documents in order to:

■ check the details of the written contents

■ check any figures

Possible mistakes include:

■ if the stock code or goods description on a purchase order are not read properly by the seller the wrong goods could be sent out

■ if a mistake in the amount sent is not detected on a remittance advice the wrong amount will most likely be entered into the accounts of the seller

REMITTANCE ADVICE		FROM: Trends 4 Friar Street Broadfield BR1 3RF	
TO Cool Socks Limited Unit 45 Elgar Estate, Broadfield, BR7 4ER		06 11 20-3	
Your ref	Our ref		Amount
787923	47609	FASTER PAYMENTS TRANSFER	254.88
		TOTAL	254.88

THIS HAS BEEN PAID BY FASTER PAYMENTS TRANSFER DIRECTLY INTO YOUR BANK ACCOUNT AT ALBION BANK NO 11451226 SO...

Is this the correct amount due according to the sales ledger account or statement?

Trends   **PURCHASE ORDER**

4 Friar Street
Broadfield
BR1 3RF
Tel 01908 761234 Fax 01908 761987
VAT REG GB 0745 8383 56

Cool Socks Limited, Unit 45 Elgar Estate, Broadfield, BR7 4ER		purchase order no date	47609 25 09 20-3
product code	quantity	description	
45B	100 pairs	Blue Toebar socks @ £2.36 per pair	

AUTHORISED signature...... *D Signer* ....date...... *25/09/20-3*

Have the product code and details been correctly transferred to the invoice?

documents received from a seller

If you are working in the finance function and deal with ordering goods and services and also for paying for them the key document you will need to check very carefully will be the Statement of Account issued by the seller. This summarises items passing through the seller's account in the Purchases Ledger of the purchaser and these should 'mirror' the items on the Statement of Account. The items to check – as shown below – will be:

■ the balance brought forward from an earlier period

■ payments made (eg Faster Payment bank transfer)

■ invoices and credit notes received

If these are all correct payment should be made according to the terms granted by the seller.

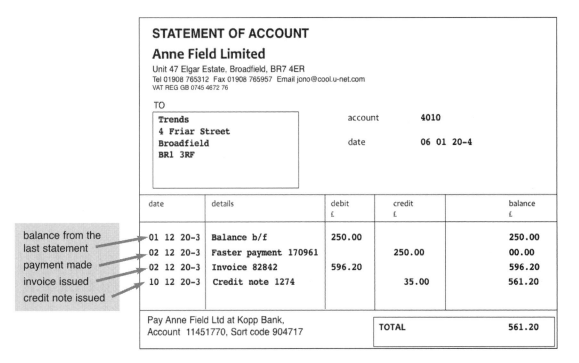

STATEMENT OF ACCOUNT

Anne Field Limited

Unit 47 Elgar Estate, Broadfield, BR7 4ER
Tel 01908 765312 Fax 01908 765957 Email jono@cool.u-net.com
VAT REG GB 0745 4672 76

TO

Trends 4 Friar Street Broadfield BR1 3RF	account	4010
	date	06 01 20-4

date	details	debit £	credit £	balance £
01 12 20-3	Balance b/f	250.00		250.00
02 12 20-3	Faster payment 170961		250.00	00.00
02 12 20-3	Invoice 82842	596.20		596.20
10 12 20-3	Credit note 1274		35.00	561.20

Pay Anne Field Ltd at Kopp Bank, Account 11451770, Sort code 904717	TOTAL	561.20

balance from the last statement
payment made
invoice issued
credit note issued

documents from other external stakeholders

Finance function staff will also have to deal with information and documents received from other external stakeholders, in paper format or electronic formats. These might include bank statements and credit card statements for company credit cards.

The bank statement extract – illustrated on the next page – is probably the most common document that finance staff will need to deal with. It is a record of the financial transactions that pass through the bank account.

United Bank plc
The Square, Broadfield, BR9 2AS

	Account title	Trends
	Account number	20963513
	Statement	49

Date	Details	Payments (debits)	Receipts (credits)	Balance
20-3				
3 Nov	Balance brought down			1,678.90 CR
10 Nov	BACS Peony Fashions 27641 **2**		1,427.85	3,106.75 CR
10 Nov	238628 **1**	249.57		2,857.18 CR
11 Nov	238629 **1**	50.00		2,807.18 CR
13 Nov	Cardline receipts **3**		267.45	3,074.63 CR
17 Nov	Transfer (Deposit A/C) **4**		400.00	3,474.63 CR
21 Nov	238630 **1**	783.90		2,690.73 CR
24 Nov	238626 **1**	127.00		2,563.73 CR
24 Nov	Albionet Websales 20963513 **3**		1,169.00	3,732.73 CR
25 Nov	DD Westmid Power **5**	589.30		3,143.43 CR
28 Nov	Bank charges **6**	87.50		3,055.93 CR

financial transactions on the bank statement

It is important that employees working in the finance function can identify items on a bank statement. Situations where this is required include:

- checking entries in the cash book of the business against the bank statement (a 'bank reconciliation statement')
- answering a query from a customer or a colleague to see if the business has received an electronic bank transfer payment the customer has made

Some of the common bank account entries (in the Details column) are listed below. The numbers shown here have been added for easy reference.

1 **cheques** – the entry in the Details column will be a number, eg '238628'

2 **electronic bank transfers received** – the entry in the Details column may contain the full details, for example: 'BACS Peony Fashions 27641'

3 **credit or debit cards payments received** – see the entries in the Details column 'Cardline receipts' and also 'Albionet Websales 20963513'

4 **internal bank transfers** – eg a transfer from a deposit account to the current account of the business – see the entry 'Transfer (Deposit A/C)'

5 **direct debit payments out** – eg paying bills or insurance premiums – see the entry 'DD Westmid Power'

6 **bank charges** – the charge made by the bank for running the account; this might be made monthly or quarterly

bank statements – the debits and credits problem

One problem for the finance staff dealing with the bookkeeping of a business is that the terms 'debit' and 'credit' are used differently by a bank and a business. In fact they are the opposite way round.

This can prove confusing when dealing with a bank statement. For a bank

- a **debit** is a **payment out** of a customer's account
- a **credit** is a **payment into** a customer's account

A business on the other hand will keep a cash book to record transactions in the bank account and in this case:

- money paid **into the bank** account in the cash book is always a **debit**
- money paid **out of the bank account** in the cash book is always a **credit**

FINANCIAL INFORMATION PRODUCED INTERNALLY

the need for internal financial information

One of the functions of the staff working in the finance function is to provide information to management so that they can monitor the financial performance of the business. The managers will then be able to make informed financial decisions about the running of the business. Examples of these types of information and the ways in which they help decision making are set out below.

sales reports

It is important that the management of a business is always made aware of the level of sales made for a range of products on at least a monthly basis. This is critical because the level of sales achieved will affect the level of profit made.

A **sales report** will enable the finance function and the sales and marketing departments to see exactly what products are doing well and which are not selling. As a result of this analysis the following decisions and recommendations could be made, depending on the circumstances:

- a **fall** in sales of Product A: increase marketing; scale down production
- an **increase** in sales of Product A: consider increasing its price (depending on the competition); increase production to meet demand

Sales reports are often set up on a spreadsheet which is updated monthly. The spreadsheet (see next page) might contain the following types of data:

- **actual** monthly sales figures per product or type of product set out in separate columns for each month
- total **cumulative** sales figures by product set out in a separate column

◇	A	B	C	D	E	F	G
1		Monthly sales report (£) 20-7					
2		January	February	March	April	May	Cumulative total
3	Product A	1,423	985	963	655	728	4,754
4	Product B	1,609	1,096	1,066	715	815	5,301
5	Product C	8,525	5,438	5,025	3,048	4,169.1	26,205
6	Product D	7,444.42	5,096.05	4,951.36	3,215.71	3,709.93	24,417
7	Product E	593.21	419.06	398.35	270.38	310.82	1,992
8	TOTAL SALES	19,594.63	13,034.11	12,403.71	7,904.09	9,732.85	62,669

unit cost reports

As you will know if you have studied the Unit 'Elements of Costing', one of the functions of the finance function is to break down the total cost of producing a product into various different costs:

■ materials used (a variable cost)

■ the cost of labour (a variable cost)

■ fixed costs (eg insurance, heating)

This information is used by the finance function to work out the total cost of producing different quantities of that product. Management can then make the decision as to how many units to produce at a time at the lowest cost per item (unit cost). It must however make sure that it can sell that number of items. For example, if a stationery business prints diaries every year there is no point in printing a very large number on the grounds that they will cost less because at the end of the year they go out of date.

In the example below if 1,000 units of an item cost £13 each to make and 1,500 units cost £11 each the business is more likely to make 1,500 units, as long as it is confident of selling them.

	A	B	C	D	E
	Comparative unit costing for 1,000 and 1,500 units (£)				
1		1,000 units		1,500 units	
2		Total Cost	Unit Cost	Total Cost	Unit Cost
3	Materials	£6,000	£6	£7,500	£5
4	Labour	£2,000	£2	£3,000	£2
5	Fixed costs	£5,000	£5	£6,000	£4
6	Total	£13,000	£13	£16,500	£11

budget reports

As you will also know if you have studied the Unit 'Elements of Costing', one role of the finance function is to plan ahead and create budgets.

A budget is a financial plan for a future period of time which estimates the likely income and costs for products made or services provided.

Budgets are useful for monitoring financial performance, answering questions like 'how well are sales performing?' or 'are our costs being kept within the planned limit?'

A critical part of the budgeting process is comparing actual performance, for example sales achieved, against the planned 'budgeted' sales. The numerical difference between the budgeted sales and the actual sales is know as a **variance**. A variance can be:

- a **favourable** (FAV) variance (a good result); this happens when
  - sales are higher than budgeted
  - costs are lower than budgeted

- an **adverse** (ADV) variance (a poor result); this happens when
  - sales are lower than budgeted
  - costs are higher than budgeted

An example of a cost budget (set up as a spreadsheet) is shown below.

	A	B	C	D	E
1		Budget £	Actual £	Variance £	Adv/Fav
2	Direct materials	60,000	64,000	4,000	Adv
3	Direct labour	24,000	25,000	1,000	Adv
4	Overheads	12,000	10,000	2,000	Fav
5	Totals	96,000	99,000	3,000	Adv

Note that:

- there are two adverse (adv) variances – direct materials were £4,000 more than budgeted and direct labour was £1,000 more than budgeted – so the business is a total of £5,000 over target

- there is only one favourable (fav) variance – this is where the actual overhead costs of £10,000 were £2,000 less than the budgeted £12,000

- the total of budgeted and actual costs are totalled to produce a net adverse (ADV) variance of £3,000

the importance of budget reports in the finance function

The importance of a budget is that it is a very useful planning tool. Managers in the finance function need to know what their **targets** are. Managers also need to **monitor** progress and so it is important that the finance staff provide them with accurate and up-to-date figures. If the performance of the business is not on target – and particularly when it is below target – the managers can then take control of the situation by carrying out actions to rectify the situation.

CASH AND TAX INFORMATION

the importance of cash

The management of a business will also want to monitor its cash position. 'Cash' in this sense includes physical cash held in the business and bank account balances. We saw in the last chapter the importance of maintaining the **solvency** of a business, ie ensuring that the business is able to pay its debts when they are due. There are a number of sources of information which are useful in providing this information:

- regular **bank statements** (see page 35); these can either be in paper format, or more often than not downloaded from the bank's website as part of the bank's online banking service

- an up-to-date **cash budget** which is drawn up for a fixed future period (eg a year) and updated monthly; this budget shows the receipts and payments of money from the business as they pass through the bank account and then calculates the balance of the bank account at the end of each month, using these figures

An example of a cash budget is shown below to give an idea of what is involved (you will not be assessed on it in this Unit). The important row of figures is the bottom one which shows the amount that the business expects to be in the bank account at the end of each month.

	January £	February £	March £	April £
Receipts				
Sales	8,500	27,500	5,000	9,000
Total Receipts **(A)**	8,500	27,500	5,000	9,000
Payments				
Purchases	3,000	22,800	3,960	3,000
Wages	2,520	5,260	1,320	1,440
Office expenses	1,800	1,800	1,800	1,800
Total Payments **(B)**	7,320	29,860	7,080	6,240
Cash flow for the month (A - B)	1,180	(2,360)	(2,080)	2,760
Bank balance b/f (beginning of month)	10,000	11,180	8,820	6,740
Bank balance c/f (end of month)	11,180	8,820	6,740	9,500

the need to pay tax on profits

Any UK business, whether sole trader, partnership or limited company, will have to pay tax on its profits. In the UK the tax authority is HM Revenue & Customs (HMRC). The type of tax paid will depend on the type of business:

- sole traders and partners have to pay **income tax** based on the profits of their business
- limited companies have to pay **corporation tax** on the profits of the company

The profit in each case is worked out in the Statement of Profit or Loss for which the finance function will provide the information. A sample Statement of Profit or Loss is shown below. You will not need to know all the workings of this financial statement for this Unit as they will be covered in full in later Units.

The important figure here is the final 'Profit for the year' which will form the basis for the tax calculation. It is basically a summary of the income (revenue) of the business less the expenses incurred during the year before the statement is drawn up.

STATEMENT OF PROFIT OR LOSS: ANNE FIELD FASHIONS
for the year ended 30 JUNE 20-7

	£000s	£000s
Sales revenue		85,500
Opening inventory	13,250	
Purchases	55,000	
	68,250	
Less Closing inventory	18,100	
Cost of sales		50,150
Gross profit		35,350
Less expenses:		
Administration expenses	1,180	
Wages	9,220	
Rent paid	1,200	
Telephone	800	
		12,400
Profit for the year		22,950

---

the need to pay tax on sales – VAT

Any UK business that sells goods or services over a certain monetary limit will need to register for **VAT** and add VAT (Value Added Tax) to sales, which will be shown on documents such as invoices and credit notes.

You will know from your study of bookkeeping that financial transactions recorded in the day books are entered into VAT Account. This account will record both VAT on sales and VAT on purchases and expenses:

■ VAT on sales will be a credit entry and **is due to HMRC**

■ VAT on purchases and expenses will be a debit entry and can be **reclaimed from HMRC**

The normal situation is that a business will have both sales and purchases to deal with and so will have:

■ VAT to pay to HMRC (on sales)

■ VAT to claim back (on purchases)

The difference between these two is the 'net VAT' and this is the amount the business will have to:

■ pay to HMRC (the most common situation) or

■ claim back from HMRC (much less common) through the VAT return

the VAT return

The normal procedure is that every three months the business will have to submit to HMRC an online **VAT return** which sets out data including:

■ VAT which is due to HMRC from sales (also known as output VAT)

■ VAT which can be reclaimed from HMRC for purchases and expenses (also known as input VAT)

■ the net VAT which is due to HMRC or is reclaimable from HMRC

the need for accuracy, completeness and being on time

Completion of the VAT return is a good example of how important it is that information provided by the finance function is complete, accurate and submitted on time.

If any of these qualities is missing, the VAT return will be defective and this could cause a lot of problems for the business. HMRC can demand penalties in serious cases where VAT returns are:

■ incomplete – eg missing important data because of an accounting error such as excluding significant amounts of VAT on sales

■ inaccurate – eg incorrect data resulting from an arithmetic error within the accounting system

■ late – ie not submitted within the required deadline

In short, it is the role of staff in the finance function to be efficient and work to a high standard in providing the required information.

THE IMPORTANCE OF DATA SECURITY

types of data

'Data' is a word which basically means 'information'. Information can be numerical or in the form of text and is normally held in two main formats: paper-based and computer-based. If you work in the finance function of an organisation such as a business you could be dealing with:

- **paper-based data** such as:
    - financial documents generated internally
    - financial documents received from customers and suppliers
    - printouts of spreadsheets
    - internal policies and procedures
    - letters

- **computer-based data** such as:
    - computer-based accounting
    - spreadsheets used for sales reports and budgeting
    - payroll
    - emails

the need for data security – confidentiality

Employees always have to take care with confidentiality of information held both in paper records and also on computers. For example:

- payroll information should always be kept strictly confidential and not revealed to other employees

- information about customers and suppliers should never be revealed to outsiders

The **Data Protection Act** is an important piece of legislation which protects the confidentiality of information about individuals. It applies to:

- personal data held on computer – eg a computer database of customer names, addresses, telephone numbers, sales details

- accessible paper-based records – eg a card index file system of customer details

You will not need to be able to quote this Act, but you should know that it states that personal data must be accurate, kept only as long as necessary and kept securely. It requires that an organisation should not reveal, without permission, personal information about its customers to other customers or any information about its employees.

DATA STORAGE

paper-based data – filing and archiving

Paper-based data, including financial documents and letters, are normally initially stored in individual files kept in filing cabinets so that they can be easily accessed. After a period of time the business will need to 'archive' them, ie store them in safe place which can be accessed if they are needed. Traditionally records of this nature are kept for six years. Sensitive data such as staff records will need to be locked and the keys only made available to senior staff.

computer-based data

Nowadays the large majority of information is processed and stored digitally. Because of the ease in which computer data can be accessed, copied and transmitted, great care must be taken to control:

- the access by staff to data
- the safe storage of data
- the protection of data against intrusion from the outside by hackers and viruses

Computer-based data will therefore require:

- the use of passwords
- secure and multiple back-up
- virus protection software

We will deal with each of these in turn.

software passwords – accessing a program

Passwords are also needed to protect sensitive and confidential data held on the computer system. This is particularly important in the areas of staff records and also in the case of financial data processed by computer accounting programs.

One solution to the problem of unauthorised employees gaining access to sensitive financial data is the use of **passwords** to gain access to a computer program.

Many larger businesses will employ a number of people who need to operate the computer accounting system; they will be issued with an appropriate password. Businesses can also set up **access rights** which restrict certain employees to certain activities and prevent them from accessing more sensitive areas such as the making of payments from the bank account.

the need for strong passwords

A safe password is known as a 'strong' password. There is no use in creating a password which is easily worked out, for example 'password' (it does happen), the name and date of birth of your partner, your favourite football team or pet rabbit. Microsoft has set out the following guidelines for a 'strong' password. It must ideally:

■ be at least eight characters long

■ not contain your user name, real name, or company name

■ not contain a complete word.

■ be significantly different from previous passwords

The password must ideally contain characters from each of the following four categories:

■ uppercase letters, eg A, B, C

■ lowercase letters, eg a, b, c

■ numbers, eg 0, 1, 2, 3, 4, 5, 6, 7, 8, 9

■ keyboard symbols, eg @ % & * _ ? /

Also it goes without saying that you should not leave your password where it is accessible, eg on a post-it note on your computer, in the front of your diary or in your phone.

backing-up files

You will also need to **back-up** the data generated by the computer. There is no set rule about when you should do this, but it should be at least at the end of every day and preferably when you have completed a long run of inputting.

back-up processes

If you are working on a network, you can normally save to your files, to your work station's hard disk and also to the server. If you have a standalone computer system, the back-up files should be saved to some form of storage device. This may take the form of:

■ a hard disk drive in the workstation itself

■ an external portable hard drive kept in the office

■ an external portable hard drive taken off the premises

Another back-up option is to back up files at a server at a remote location or direct to the 'cloud'.

It is important that an organisation works out a systematic policy for back-up of its data. This could involve:

■ daily back-ups held both on and off the premises

■ a 'time machine' hard drive which records and stores files at regular short intervals – in other words it will enable you to go 'back in time' to recover files at an earlier stage of production if a file becomes corrupted or accidentally deleted

anti-virus software

Anti-virus software is a 'must' for any organisation such as a business which uses the internet. This software, also known as **anti-malware** software, is computer software which is used to set up an effective shield against intrusive and destructive **malware** which can wipe your files, disable your software and then spread via the internet to other computer users. Malware should be kept at bay at all costs.

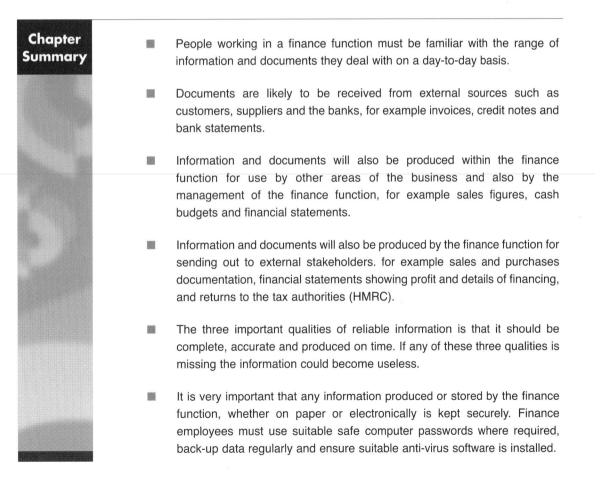

Chapter Summary

■ People working in a finance function must be familiar with the range of information and documents they deal with on a day-to-day basis.

■ Documents are likely to be received from external sources such as customers, suppliers and the banks, for example invoices, credit notes and bank statements.

■ Information and documents will also be produced within the finance function for use by other areas of the business and also by the management of the finance function, for example sales figures, cash budgets and financial statements.

■ Information and documents will also be produced by the finance function for sending out to external stakeholders. for example sales and purchases documentation, financial statements showing profit and details of financing, and returns to the tax authorities (HMRC).

■ The three important qualities of reliable information is that it should be complete, accurate and produced on time. If any of these three qualities is missing the information could become useless.

■ It is very important that any information produced or stored by the finance function, whether on paper or electronically is kept securely. Finance employees must use suitable safe computer passwords where required, back-up data regularly and ensure suitable anti-virus software is installed.

Key Terms	**debits and credits**	a bank statement shows **debits** as **payments out** of the bank account and **credits** as **payments into** the bank account; this is opposite to the treatment of bank transactions in the cash book of a business where money received is a debit and money paid out is a credit
	sales report	a schedule produced by the finance function showing sales by product or product range by month, set up as a report for management, often on a spreadsheet
	unit cost report	a report produced by the finance function which breaks down for management the total cost of producing a product into material, labour and fixed costs
	budget	a financial plan produced by the finance function for a future period of time; it estimates the likely income and costs of products made or services provided
	cash budget	a forecast produced by the finance function showing the receipts and payments of money through the bank account of a business and the way in which they affect the bank balance each month
	statement of profit or loss	a financial statement produced by the finance function which deducts the costs of a business from its revenue in order to calculate its profit which will then be subject to tax
	VAT Return	a regular report to HM Revenue & Customs (HMRC) prepared by the financial function setting out the total VAT received from customer sales and the total VAT paid out to suppliers on purchases so that the amount of VAT due can be calculated
	data security	the need to keep personal data held by a business securely and confidentially
	Data Protection Act	the law which sets out how personal data held by a business should be held securely and confidentially
	archiving	the process of storing data securely over a period of time so that it can be easily accessed
	passwords	a unique mixture of characters (ie letters, numbers and symbols) which can give access by employees to computer systems; used for keeping data safe and confidential

Activities

3.1   It is important to check a remittance advice when it is received because:

(a)	There might be an error with a stock code quoted, resulting in the wrong goods being supplied	
(b)	The total may not agree with the total on the statement of account sent by the seller	
(c)	The wrong VAT rate may have been applied on the invoice sent	

Tick the **one** correct option.

3.2   It is important for a seller to check a purchase order for goods when it is received because:

(a)	The product code may not agree with the description of the goods and so it will need to be queried	
(b)	The total may not agree with the total on the statement of account sent by the seller	
(c)	It does not include a VAT calculation	

Tick the **one** correct option.

3.3   It is important for a business that has bought goods to check a statement of account issued by the seller because:

(a)	The VAT amounts will need to be recorded in the ledgers	
(b)	The amounts sent by the buyer in settlement of invoices must be correctly shown on the statement	
(c)	It might include bank charges which will need looking into	

Tick the **one** correct option.

3.4   Complete the following two sentences by using the correct terms set out in bold print below.

debit   **credit**

A bank will refer to money paid into the bank as a [   ] and a business using a

cash book to record payments in will treat a payment received as a [   ].

A bank will refer to a payment out of a bank account as a [   ] and a business

using a cash book to record a payment made from the bank account as a [   ].

3.5   Complete the two sentences below using the following phrases:

sales are higher than budgeted   **sales are lower than budgeted**

costs are lower than budgeted   **costs are higher than budgeted**

A favourable variance occurs when [   ]

or [   ].

An adverse variance occurs when [   ]

or [   ].

3.6   A business is most likely to be able to manage its cash position effectively by:

(a)	Filing its bank statements safely and confidentially	
(b)	Maximising the number of payments made by electronic transfer	
(c)	Drawing up a cash budget	

Tick the **one** correct option.

3.7   A business will be able to calculate the amount of tax it has to pay by drawing up:

(a)	A unit cost report	
(b)	A statement of profit or loss	

Tick the **one** correct option.

3.8   Keeping confidentiality within a business means:

(a)	Keeping data backed up in more than one format	
(b)	Being truthful and honest in your dealings	
(c)	Not releasing personal data to outsiders	

Tick the **one** correct option.

3.9   Creating passwords for accessing software require that the password must be 'strong' and not easily broken (guessed). List the following four passwords in order of strength (ie the strongest password first).

mypassword   **pass2A%**   **kith33**   **G5Thrones**

1	
2	
3	
4	

3.10   Backing up of computer data within a business should ideally be carried out:

(a)	At least daily	
(b)	In more than one storage format	
(c)	And stored only on the premises	
(d)	And only stored externally	
(e)	And stored on the premises and also externally	

Tick the correct options.

4 Effective business communications

this chapter covers...

This chapter explains the need for people working in the finance function to be able to communicate with work colleagues and also with people outside the workplace – customers and suppliers, for example.

- *Effective communication needs to be:*
  - *clear, structured and presented logically*
  - *appropriate to the situation and easily understood*
  - *accurate and technically correct*

- *Communication may be:*
  - *internal within the business or external, eg with customers and suppliers*
  - *verbal or written*
  - *presented on paper or processed on a computer*

- *The specific types of communication covered in this chapter include:*
  - *business letters*
  - *emails*
  - *faxes*
  - *written notes*
  - *business reports*

- *The language used in business communications is generally more formal than everyday language used with friends and family*

Note: *people working in the finance function will also use their communication skills to present numbers and calculations, often using spreadsheets. This will be covered in the next chapter.*

THE NEED TO COMMUNICATE

the need for effective communication

If you are communicating a message to another person or group of people, that message must be **effective** to be successful. The message must achieve its aim and be:

■ clear and easily understood – concise and expressed in unambiguous language

■ correct – there is no point in unintentionally misleading people

■ provided at the right time – not too early and not too late

On a personal level, if you are organising a meal out with a group of friends, you will need to email, phone or text instructions giving clear details of the place, date and time and asking for confirmation. You need to provide this information in good time and be available to receive replies. This is a very basic comparison, but the same principles apply to any workplace situation.

forms of communication – the people involved

Communication can be very varied. If you consider a working day and compile a log of all the forms of communication you get involved in you would find that you would be recording:

■ **internal communications** – with colleagues, line managers and anyone else involved in your reporting lines

■ **external communications** – depending on your role in the organisation, this could be with customers, suppliers, the bank, carriers and the local sandwich or pizza delivery company

If you are communicating **within the organisation** you should

■ choose the most appropriate method

■ be polite – even if you do not feel like it at the time

■ act promptly – do not leave things to later, they may never happen

If you are communicating **with outsiders** you should

■ choose the most appropriate method of communication

■ communicate clearly, accurately and promptly

■ present a professional approach

■ comply with 'corporate image' – this may mean using standard letters and forms, or speaking on the telephone using standard 'scripts'

forms of communication – the methods used

There are many methods of communication that can be used. There is normally a clear choice for most circumstances, although occasionally it can be effective if a normally accepted method is changed if the circumstances demand it. For example, a telephone call may be more effective than yet another unanswered email in dealing with a potential problem, communication being better than silence.

The choice of communication methods used involve a number of classifications:

■ **verbal** or **written** methods of communication:

    – verbal: telephone calls, voicemail messages, in-house, meetings, conference calls

    – written: business letters, reports, notes

■ written communication can be **paper-based** or **electronic:**

    – paper-based: letters, notes, reports

    – electronic: emails, texts on a mobile, scanned documents

The choice will normally be based on custom, ie 'what is normally done'. The variety of possible methods is shown in the diagram set out below.

In the rest of the chapter we will describe some of the more common communication methods – including business letters, emails, notes for verbal messages and business reports.

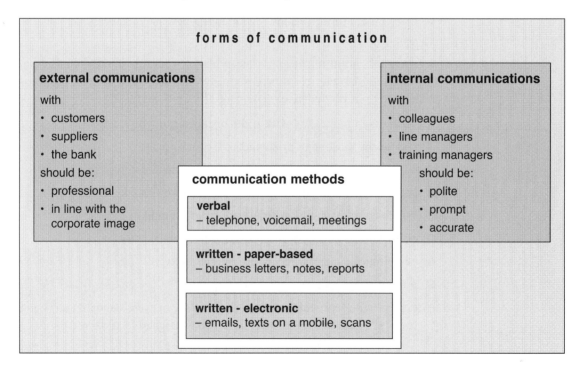

BUSINESS LETTERS

When you deal with business letters you will see that the appearance and format of each letter is in a uniform 'house' style, a style which identifies that business, and is common to all letters that it sends. The letter will normally be on standard printed stationery showing the name, address and details of the business, and will be set out with headings, paragraphs, signatures – the 'elements' of the letter – in a uniform way.

There are a number of different ways of setting out the text of a letter. The most common of these used in business is illustrated and explained on the next two pages.

characteristics of a business letter

The most commonly letter format is known as a 'fully blocked' style:

- all the lines start at the left margin

- the use of open punctuation, ie there is no punctuation, except in the main body of the letter, which uses normal punctuation

- paragraphs are divided by a space, and are not indented

- a fully blocked letter is easy to key in as all the lines are set uniformly to the left margin

elements of the letter

The explanations which follow refer to the letter shown on page 55.

printed letterhead   The name and address of the business is normally printed on the paper, and must be up-to-date.

reference   The reference on the letter illustrated (DH/SB/69) is a standard format:
- DH (Derek Hunt), the writer
- SB (Sally Burgess), the secretary
- 69, the number of the file where the correspondence is kept

If you need to quote the reference of a letter to which you are replying, the references will be quoted as follows: Your ref TR/FG/45 Our ref DH/SB/69.

date	The date is entered in date (number), month (word), year (number) order.
recipient	The name and address of the person to whom the letter is sent. This section of the letter may be displayed in the window of a window envelope, so it is essential that it is accurate.
salutation	'Dear Sir. . . Dear Madam' – if you know the person's name and title (ie Mr, Mrs, Miss, Ms) use it, but check that it is correct – a misspelt name or an incorrect title will ruin an otherwise competent letter.
heading	The heading sets out the subject matter of the letter – it will concentrate the reader's mind.
body	The body of the letter is an area where the message of the letter is set out. The text must:

– be laid out in short precise paragraphs and short clear sentences

– start with a point of reference (eg referring to an invoice)

– set out the message in a logical sequence

– be written in plain English – but avoid 'slang' expressions and, equally, avoid unusual or old-fashioned words which obscure the meaning

– finish with a clear indication of the next step to be taken (eg please telephone, please arrange appointment, please buy our products, please pay our invoice)

complimentary close	The complimentary close (signing off phrase) must be consistent with the salutation:

'Dear Sir/Dear Madam' followed by 'Yours faithfully'

'Dear Mr Sutton/Dear Ms Jones' followed by 'Yours sincerely'.

name and job title	It is essential for the reader to know the name of the person who sent the letter, and that person's job title, because a reply will need to be addressed to a specific person.
enclosures	If there are enclosures with the letter, the abbreviation 'enc' or 'encl' is used at the bottom of the letter.

the 'house style' letter

Wyvern Motor Supplies
107 High Street
Mereford
MR1 9SZ
Tel 01605 675365   Fax 01605 765576   Email sales@WMSupplies.co.uk

reference → Ref DH/SB/69

date → 15 December 20-7

name and address of recipient →
Purchasing Department
Osborne Car Accessories
17 Pump Street
Mereford MR6 7ER

salutation → Dear Sir

heading → Invoice 8288 £10,589.50

body of the letter →
We note from our records that we have not yet received payment of our invoice 8288 dated 15 September 20-7. Our up-to-date statement of account is enclosed, together with a copy of the invoice.

Our payment terms are strictly 30 days from the date of the invoice. We shall be grateful if you will settle the £10,589.50 without further delay.

We look forward to receiving your payment.

complimentary close → Yours faithfully

signature → *D M Hunt*

name and job title →
Derek Hunt
Accounts Manager

enclosures → enc

EMAILS

'netiquette' - the art of email writing

Email is an increasingly common form of written communication. There is an accepted set of rules of 'what to do' and 'what not to do' when writing a business email; this is sometimes referred to as 'netiquette.' If you work for an organisation you must ensure that you are familiar with the ways in which emails are written and dealt with. It is essential that you always project a professional image of your organisation when composing and replying to an email.

Although professional emails are seen as being more informal than letters, there is no excuse for careless mistakes, use of texting language, emoticons (eg smileys), LOTS OF CAPITAL LETTERS and exclamation marks!!!!!!!

Study the email shown below and then read the hints that follow.

Send	Chat	Attach	Address	Fonts	Colors	Save As Draft

To: james.wilson@goodcommunications.co.uk

Cc:

Subject: Good practice in emailing

Dear James

I thought you might like the attached list of points to be observed when writing good emails.

Many of these points may seem obvious but you would be surprised to see how many times they are ignored.

I would be interested to get your feedback.

kind regards

Reeta Mayde

Apix Promotions Limited
Registered in England at Unit 19 Maxwell Estate, Yarmouth Road, Oldborough, CL2 8BK
Company No 4356859
VAT No 154 6106 99

recipient

It is obviously important to get the email address right.

subject

Keep the subject description short and to the point. Use a capital letter for the start of the first word.

Cc

The 'Cc' (carbon copy) is used to send a message to a group of people, and each person in the group who receives the message will see the addresses of the others in the list. These people should therefore ideally know each other. 'Cc' should only be used if you are happy that they are all aware that the others on the list are receiving the message. If it is used to send a message to a group of strangers you may annoy them and breach privacy regulations.

Bcc

'Bcc' (blind carbon copy) is an option (not shown on the illustration) which can be used to email a group of contacts who do not know each other. 'Bcc' allows the message to go to a group, but the group members do not know that it is a group mailing as they do not see the details of the other recipients.

addressing the recipient

How do you address your new contacts? It all depends on the relationship. If the person is well known to you, the usual 'Hi Ramjit,' 'Hello Laura,' is quite acceptable. The approach is very similar to a telephone call. If you do not know the recipient you should be very formal: 'Dear Mr Lubowski,' 'Dear Ms. Terry,' and so on. You should remain on formal terms until in due course it is clear from the other person that you can say 'Hi Sue,' or whatever is required.

signing off

On the whole you should use the same process as you would if you were writing a business letter. If you start with 'Dear Mr Brown' you should finish with 'Yours sincerely' although there is a tendency now also to use 'kind regards' or 'best wishes' instead.

how formal should the text be?

An email is different from a letter in this respect. The level of formality will depend on the relationship with the recipient. Whatever the level of formality, an email should have correct spelling, grammar and punctuation. Ideally, sentences should be short and separated into distinct paragraphs.

It makes the message clearer if you put a blank line between paragraphs.

If it is an **internal** email, a degree of informality is more normal – eg 'Hi Jon,' 'Regards, Mike' and so on. In practice close colleagues will sometimes abbreviate even further – eg 'John, the Huxborough contract needs signing. Thanks. Geoff.'

some email do's and do nots

Do . . .

- keep the message short and to the point
- when replying, answer the points raised in the incoming message
- reply or confirm receipt of the message on the same day
- read through and edit what you have written before you send it
- make sure the original message 'thread' is included when replying

Do not . . .

- use text in CAPITAL LETTERS - THIS IS KNOWN AS 'SHOUTING'
- use too much fancy formatting, eg underlines, different fonts, bright colours – they may be lost when the message is printed out by the recipient
- send large attachments which might clog up the recipient's email system
- say something in an email that you would not say to someone's face

FAXES AND SCANS

The fax (short for 'facsimile') enables you to transmit electronically an exact copy of the details on a sheet of paper. This can either be done on a computer or on a fax machine. If you use a fax machine you feed the sheet into the machine, dial up the recipient on the inbuilt telephone pad and transmit the document down the line. The machine at the other end will print out an exact copy of the original document.

The fax can be used within an organisation or for external contact with a customer. You sometimes send a 'fax header' first sheet (see illustration on the next page) and then feed in any further pages/documents as required.

The fax is very useful for sending copies of documents. A frequent excuse given by people who are slow at paying is "I can't pay because I don't seem to have the original invoice". This can be replied to with "No problem! We can fax you a copy. What is your fax number?" Look at the example on the next page.

Note that the fax is less commonly used nowadays. It is often easier to email the message and attach a scan or pdf of any document (or documents) that the recipient needs.

Winterborn Electronics Limited

Unit 4 Everoak Estate, Bromyard Road
St Johns, Worcester WR2 5HN
tel 01905 748043 fax 01905 748911

facsimile transmission header

To: Jamie Milne, Accounts Office, Zippo Computers

Fax number: 01350 525504

Number of pages including this header: 2   Date: 17 October 20-7

message

Invoice 24375

Further to our recent telephone conversation I am faxing you a copy of invoice 24375 which is now overdue.

I shall be grateful if you will arrange for the £4,678.50 owing to be paid to us by bank transfer within the next seven days.

R Pound

Credit Controller

NOTES

notes to others

A traditional form of communication within an organisation is the written **note**. This can be:

- an informal written note, passing on a message or an instruction

- a telephone message you pass on to a colleague (some organisations use preprinted telephone message pads)

The important elements of a written note are:

- the name of the person who is sending the note

- the name of the person who is to receive the note

- the time and date that the note is written

- a clearly stated message

- a clear indication of any action to be taken as a result of the message

Note how the examples of notes on the next page contain all these elements.

To Tim Blackstock,
Order Processing

Please remember to allow PDT Ltd an
extra 10% trade discount on invoices
this month.

John Tregennick, Sales
03.04.-7   10.30

TELEPHONE MESSAGE

TO   Karin Schmidt, Accounts
FROM   H Khan, Sales
DATE   22 April 20-7
TIME   12.30

Please ring Jim Stoat at RF Electronics –
he is complaining that they have not
received a credit note for returned
damaged inventory (order ref 823423).
Please treat urgently – he is not happy!

HK

Nowadays **internal email** is becoming more a common method for passing on messages and making requests electronically within an office, but this does rely on the person to whom the message is written picking up the email in time. A written note placed prominently on the recipient's desk or placed on a computer keyboard can sometimes have a much more immediate effect.

lists and notes to yourself

It is common practice in everyday life to summarise in note form 'things that have to be done', for example compiling a shopping list or a list of jobs for the weekend. The memory is not always totally reliable in this respect.

There are instances at work where you may have to do the same sort of thing thing, for example a daily 'to do' list.

It may also be possible that you have to prepare for some form of **verbal communication** that is required, for example:

■ a 'report back' to an internal meeting of a subject you have been asked to look into, eg the levels of discount given by your competitors

■ an explanation of a new office procedure to other staff

■ a list of topics to bring up at a staff appraisal, eg performance, promotion and pay

■ an important phone call to a customer about a complex technical issue

In each case each item on the list you compile should ideally be:

■ clear, short and to the point, not too wordy

■ preceded by numbers or bullet points

■ set out in a logical order

TYPES OF REPORT

who needs written reports?

A written report is a way of informing a person or a group of people about a specific subject. A report is a structured way of communicating complex information and can vary in length, complexity and importance. Reports can be:

- short or extended
- formal or informal
- routine or 'one-off'
- internal or external

It all depends on who is going to read it and how important it is. Examples of a less complex **routine report** include:

- a monthly sales report for internal management analysing sales figures by product and region
- a monthly report for management setting out the overtime worked by employees in the various departments of the business

A less formal report may just have a title, date, the name of the person/department that prepared it, the information provided and comments.

Examples of a more complex and formal **'one-off' report** include:

- a **report** to investigate, discuss and decide on specific **policy** issues, for example an assessment of changes to the accounting system, the paying of bonuses, the possibility of exporting products
- a report prepared for a business by outside consultants, eg on health and safety requirements

contents of a formal business report

A more complex formal report will have the following sections (note that they are numbered):

> Title Page
> 1 Summary (Executive Summary)
> 2 Introduction
> 3 Findings
> 4 Conclusions
> 5 Recommendations
> 6 Appendices

REPORT FORMAT

We will describe each of the sections of a report in turn.

Title page

The report will normally be headed up with a single page setting out:

■ details of the person/people it is being sent to (including job title)

■ the person who has prepared the report (including job title)

■ the date

■ the title of the report

For example:

> To: Josh Khan, Accounts Manager
>
> From: A Student, Accounts Assistant, Sales Ledger
>
> Date: 5 February 20-7
>
> REPORT ON OVERDUE CUSTOMER ACCOUNTS

1 Summary

This section is also sometimes known as an **executive summary** because it is written for rapid reading by management (the 'executives'). It may take up less than a page. The summary will be brief and will set out:

■ the subject matter of the report – in this case customers who have not settled their accounts on time

■ what the report covers – the findings of the investigation into overdue debts

■ conclusion(s) of the report – brief details and assessment of the findings

■ what the report recommends – identification of the debts that should be written off

2 Introduction

This will state:

■ the nature of the task set and the date when it was set

■ the person who set the task

■ the deadline for the task

See the next page for an example of how the Introduction might read.

> **2   Introduction**
>
> 2.1   On 30 January a request was made for:
>
> - an investigation into sales ledger accounts that were outstanding for more than six months later than the due date
>
> - the provision of a list and details of all overdue amounts
>
> 2.2   This report was to be completed by 7 February.

Note that the decimal system of numbering is used. This means that this second section of the report is the Introduction and . . .

■ it is given the identifying number '2'

■ the sub-sections of the Introduction are referenced with the numbers '2.1' and '2.2'. If there had been a third it would have been '2.3'.

3   Findings (Main Body)

The third section of the report contains the 'Findings'. This is the **main body** of the report and sets out all the information gathered together as a result of the investigation. It lists sources of information and presents the findings in a clear and logical way.

A table could be incorporated to set out data. If a computer spreadsheet program is used it will give a professional appearance to the report (see the next chapter for the use of spreadsheets). If the findings include a large amount of data or printouts, they should be included in an Appendix and referred to in the main text.

> **3   Findings**
>
> 3.1   The information gathered for this report has been taken from:
>
> - Sales Ledger accounts
>
> - copies of relevant correspondence relating to the overdue accounts
>
> 3.2   A detailed list showing the accounts overdue more than six months is set out below.

4   Conclusions

The conclusions should be based entirely on the 'Findings' and should not introduce any other factors or information. This section of the report could begin as follows:

4	**Conclusions**
4.1	The figures and the correspondence in the Findings indicate that it is unlikely that the Finance Department will be able to recover the following customer debts:
	. . . (a list of the relevant accounts and amounts would be entered)

5   Recommendations

The recommendations are the actions that should be taken as a result of the conclusions reached in the previous section of the report. For example, in the case of the irrecoverable debts:

5	**Recommendations**
5.1	It is recommended that the following accounts should be chased up and Court Action threatened.

Sometimes, if the conclusions are brief and straightforward it makes sense to combine the 'Conclusions' and 'Recommendations' sections. But for your assessment, you should assume that they will be separate.

6   Appendices

This final section of a report will include the reference material which is too bulky to include in the main 'Findings' section. In the irrecoverable debt example in this chapter this could include lists of account balances and Aged Trade Receivable Analyses.

6	**Appendices**
6.1	Sales Ledger account balances (as at 31 January 20-7).

The diagram below summarises the process of putting a Business Report together.

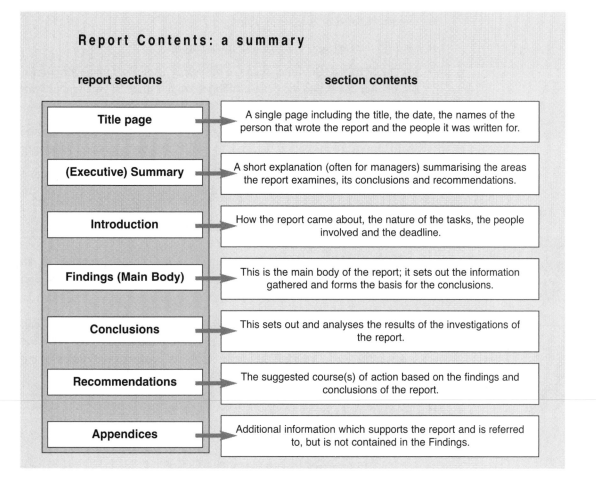

Report Contents: a summary

report sections	section contents
Title page	A single page including the title, the date, the names of the person that wrote the report and the people it was written for.
(Executive) Summary	A short explanation (often for managers) summarising the areas the report examines, its conclusions and recommendations.
Introduction	How the report came about, the nature of the tasks, the people involved and the deadline.
Findings (Main Body)	This is the main body of the report; it sets out the information gathered and forms the basis for the conclusions.
Conclusions	This sets out and analyses the results of the investigations of the report.
Recommendations	The suggested course(s) of action based on the findings and conclusions of the report.
Appendices	Additional information which supports the report and is referred to, but is not contained in the Findings.

REPORT LANGUAGE AND STYLE

A report requires straightforward written English. There is nothing particularly difficult about producing written English; the problems lie with the tendency to write as you speak, or as you text, email to friends or post on Facebook. The result is often an abbreviated form of written English which as you will appreci8 does nt work 2 well on the page.

Another problem facing people who are not used to writing formal written English is that they think of it as some sort of overblown 'posh' sounding language which has to be complicated and impressive to make its point. Nothing could be further from the truth. The test of good written English is that it should be plain and simple.

some hints on writing plain English in a report

■ use **simple words** instead of complicated ones

■ use **short sentences** instead of long ones

■ split up the text into manageable **paragraphs**

■ use the **active tense** rather than the passive, eg 'the line manager *carries out* regular checks on the petty cash book' rather than 'regular checks *are carried out* on the petty cash book by the line manager'

■ **avoid slang** eg 'the manager was really *hacked off*'; you should use the word 'annoyed' instead of 'hacked' to avoid the innocent reader assuming that the manager has suffered some terrible injury

■ avoid **abbreviations** such as 'isn't', didn't' and write the phrases in full: 'is not' and 'did not'

Chapter Summary

■ Effective **communication** is essential to the efficient running of an organisation. Any message must be easily understood, correct and communicated on time.

■ Communication in an organisation can be **internal** (with colleagues) and **external** (eg with customers). It is important that all external communications, whatever the format, give a **professional image** of the organisation.

■ There are many different types of communication, all used for very specific purposes, for example:

– verbal and written communications

– paper-based and electronic communications

■ The main **verbal communications** are telephone and voicemail messages, and discussions in meetings.

■ The main **written communications** are business letters, notes and reports (all paper-based) and emails, text messages, faxes and scans (electronic messages).

■ The main sections of a business **report** are:
– title page
– summary (also known as an executive summary)
– introduction
– findings (main body)
– conclusions
– recommendations
– appendices

business letter	a formal paper document, drawn up in a specific 'house style,' used for a wide range of purposes and normally posted to the recipient
email	a form of electronic communication with a unique set of procedures, different from letter writing
netiquette	the rules for writing emails which must be strictly observed if an organisation is to maintain a professional image
fax	the process in which a paper document is scanned and sent electronically to the recipient
note	a simple written message used within an organisation to pass on information, make a request or enable an employee to prepare a verbal communication
business report	a structured document used to communicate complex information and recommendations following an investigation and/or analysis

Activities

4.1 Which **one** of the following four options is the most important for creating an effective communication? Tick the correct option.

(a)	The message must be clear and in writing	
(b)	The message must be clear and correct	
(c)	The message must be clear and on time	
(d)	The message must be clear, correct and on time	

4.2 Its or It's? Study the four sentences below and tick the **two** correct options.

(a)	Its rubbish weather today	
(b)	It's rubbish weather today	
(c)	I do not like this film; it's not one of the best Bond films	
(d)	I do not like this film; its not one of the best Bond films	

4.3 'There', 'their' or 'they're'? Study the three sentences below and if you think any of them is wrong, write the correct word in the right-hand column.

(a)	Politicians are corrupt. Their all the same	
(b)	The students forgot there calculators for the assessment	
(c)	They're are sensible students who brought calculators	

4.4 A senior colleague has been compiling a report for management. He has written each section of the report in a separate Word file and has emailed you seven files which appear to be in the wrong order. The file names are shown below in the boxes on the left. You are to write the file names in the boxes on the right in the correct order, starting with the first file name at the top.

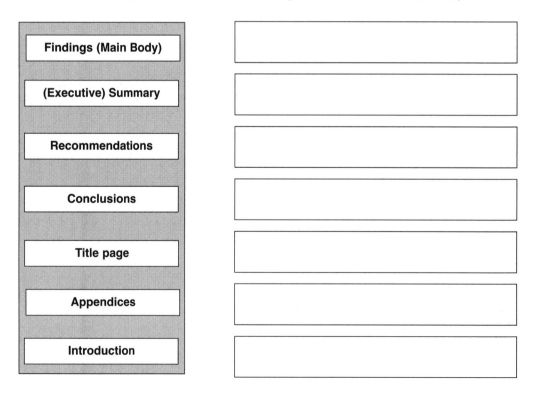

Findings (Main Body)
(Executive) Summary
Recommendations
Conclusions
Title page
Appendices
Introduction

4.5   You have been passed the following draft letter (to a Miss Coleman) to check. The letter concerns Order No 239847224. It has not yet been signed.

There are five major errors which could include wrong spellings, bad grammar or wrong use of words.

You are to:

(a)   Identify the five incorrect words and enter them in the left-hand column of the table below.

(b)   Enter your correction of these five words on the appropriate line in the right-hand column of the table below.

Dear Mrs Colman,

<u>Refund for faulty goods (Order Ref 239847244)</u>

We are sorry that you are dissappointed with the goods you ordered from us on 5 September.

They're are two possible solutions to the problem: we can make a refund on your credit card account or issue you with a credit note.

Please let us know which course of action you would like us to take.

Yours faithfully,

Incorrect word	Correction

4.6   Your name is Jamie and you work as an assistant in the Accounts Department of Frankie's Fashionware and have been passed the draft email (shown below) to complete.

The email is a request to Laura Wood (l.wood@frankiesfashionware.co.uk), an assistant in the Sales Department, to provide details of 'St Tropez shades (code 9424)' sold during the month of June. You need the information by 9 July. **You are to:**

(a)   Insert the email address of the recipient in the appropriate box.

(b)   Complete the remaining boxes (they are numbered for reference) with the most appropriate words or phrases from the lists shown below (also numbered for reference).

From   j.mason@frankiesfashionware.co.uk

To   _____

Subject   _____ [1]

Hi Laura

Please send me the quantity of _____ [2] sold

during the month of _____ [3] . We need this information to carry

out a costing exercise. I need the information, please, by _____ [4] .

Many thanks and kind regards

Jamie

Accounts Department

Option Lists

Pick one word or phrase for each numbered box from the following numbered lists:

1   Sales data for June, June data, Tropez data, Shades

2   St Tropez shades (code 9242), St Tropez shades (code 9424), St Tropez shades

3   July, August, June, September

4   9 June, 2 August, 9 July, 9 August

4.7 The following two notes were written within the finance function of a business. In each case identify and write down two important elements that are missing.

(a)

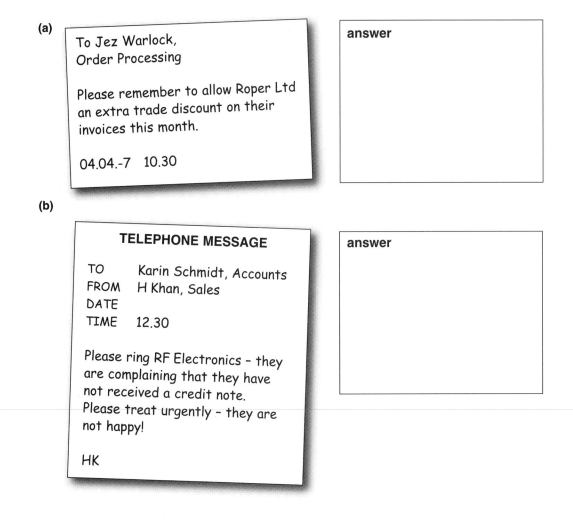

To Jez Warlock,
Order Processing

Please remember to allow Roper Ltd
an extra trade discount on their
invoices this month.

04.04.-7 10.30

answer

(b)

TELEPHONE MESSAGE

TO   Karin Schmidt, Accounts
FROM   H Khan, Sales
DATE
TIME   12.30

Please ring RF Electronics – they
are complaining that they have
not received a credit note.
Please treat urgently – they are
not happy!

HK

answer

4.8 Give examples of three situations in which an employee might write down notes in preparation for a conversation they have to make or a presentation they have to give.

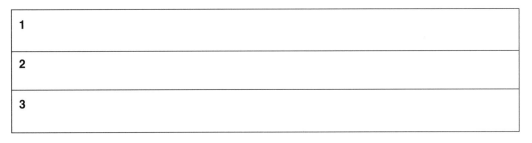

1	
2	
3	

5 Calculations and spreadsheets

this chapter covers...

This chapter is a practical guide showing you how to carry out the types of basic calculation that you are likely to encounter when working in a finance function using a calculator and in some cases, spreadsheets.

These techniques include:

■ *carrying out calculations and using estimation to check what you have done*

■ *converting numbers in words into figures*

■ *using addition, subtraction, multiplication and division*

■ *understanding proportions, ie parts of a whole, which form the basis of*

   – *fractions to express the part of a whole*

   – *percentages, a common function used in finance to calculate a variety of figures*

   – *ratios which express the numerical relationship of the parts that make up a whole*

■ *dealing with averages, for example calculating the average value of inventory held by a business*

■ *using tables to present numbers*

■ *using formulas in spreadsheets to make calculations automatically*

■ *using spreadsheets to create different types of graphs and charts which can be used in reports to illustrate numbers, proportions and trends*

BASIC CALCULATIONS

processing of numerical data

Working in finance often involves processing large volumes of figures. This may be carried out using electronic aids:

- a calculator used for various numerical functions such as addition, subtraction, multiplication and division

- a spreadsheet for processing a budget

- a computer accounting program for calculating invoice totals

accurate checking of data – estimation

In all these cases accuracy of **input** of the figures is very important and should be routinely **checked** as part of the office procedures. In the case of the addition of columns of figures, one way of checking accuracy is to carry out the procedure twice, and get somebody else to call out the figures if there is a discrepancy.

Estimation is also very important when you carry out or check a calculation. Does the total seem about right? Common sense is critical. For example, does the admin office really need to order 2,500 pens, or should it be 25?

The situation below is based on a real incident and shows the serious danger of not using common sense or checking figures properly.

Online Electronics store apologises for 49p TV error

Thousands of internet shoppers who bought a TV normally priced at £499 but quoted at an online price of 49p have been told the deal was too good to be true.

The internet store is refusing to honour the website deals and has apologised, saying the mistake in pricing was down to a "genuine internal error".

About 10,000 customers had bought the 32" TV over a Bank Holiday.

But the company has now cancelled all the orders and is giving refunds.

A company spokesperson commented that this problem was down to an unfortunate mistake "while keying in data".

converting words into numbers

Another basic numeracy skill is the ability to convert numbers written in word form into actual numbers, for example:

10.5 million = 10,500,000

This is straightforward, but it is important to appreciate that some of the larger numbers are less well known. One billion, for example is normally expressed as a thousand million. The UK National debt (ie what the UK government has borrowed) at the time of writing was an immense £1,670 billion:

£1,670 billion = £1,670,000,000,000

It is rather unlikely that you will be dealing with figures of this size, but it is a basic numeracy skill to know the meaning of this terminology.

addition

Adding a series of figures is very straightforward in principle, but care needs to be taken:

■ when dealing with figures with a decimal point – sometimes the number of decimal places varies, for example:

45.6 + 67.98 + 95 = 208.58

■ when dealing with figures which vary in size, for example:

23,567 + 74,349,117 + 76 = 74,372,760

As mentioned before, it is good practice to carry out all calculations twice to check for accuracy and then, if possible, get them checked.

subtraction and addition

The process of subtraction is similar to that of addition except that you are deducting figures rather than adding them.

Fortunately the calculator with its '+' and '–' function keys will deal automatically with more complex calculations which involve subtraction, or sometimes a mix of addition and subtraction. For example

■ combining two negative figures, eg

– 2 *minus* – 2 *equals* 0

■ combining a negative figure and a positive figure, eg

– 20 *plus* + 40 *equals* 20

Again, it is good practice to carry out all calculations twice and get them checked.

using multiplication and division

Multiplication is commonly used when checking invoices. For example, if you receive an order for 10 red box files which cost £4.00 each, you will produce an invoice which will show: **product quantity x unit price,** ie

$$10 \ \text{x} \ \pounds4.00 \ = \ \pounds40.00$$

This is straightforward enough; you just need to make the calculation and check it and apply the estimation test. Does £40 seem a reasonable answer?

Division can be seen as the opposite of multiplication. Division works out how many times one number is contained in another number. For example if a business receives 12 bottles of wine as a present and they have to be shared equally by 6 employees, the answer is that they will receive 2 bottles each. The calculation here is very simple:

$$12 \ \div \ 6 \ = \ 2 \ \text{bottles each}$$

Division is commonly used in accounting when working out the cost of a product: the cost is divided by the number of units to produce a unit cost. Division also forms the basis of fraction and percentage calculations, as will be explained on the next few pages.

understanding proportions

a proportion is a part of a whole in relation to the whole

The concept of **proportion** forms the basis of fractions, percentages and ratios, which will be explained in the next couple of pages.

For example, if it is shown that for every five trains that arrive at a certain station, one is late, you can say that the proportion of trains that arrive late is 'one in five'

fractions

A fraction is used to express a part of a whole (unit)

The calculation of a fraction, as stated above, is based on the concept of proportion.

- an example of a fraction is $3/4$

- the number above the line (the numerator) is the number of parts involved – here it is 3 parts

- the number below the line (the denominator) is the number of equal parts into which the unit is divided – here it is 4 parts

calculations using fractions

If you need to work out a 'part of a whole' using a fraction you:

■ multiply the whole amount by the number on the top of the fraction

■ divide the result of this by the number on the bottom of the fraction

For example, if you need to work out $^3/4$ of £12.00 the calculation is:

■ 3 (ie the number on the top of the fraction) x £12.00 = £36.00

■ £36.00 ÷ 4 (ie the number on the bottom of the fraction) = £9.00

So $^3/4$ of £12.00 is £9.00.

As a fraction is a 'part of a whole' it can be used to calculate a sum of money which is included in a total amount. For example, you may want to know how much VAT charged at 20% is included in a £24 purchase so that you can enter the VAT in the accounts. The fraction used here is $^1/6$. This is known as the 'VAT fraction'. The calculation is:

$$\frac{1}{6} \ \times \ £24 \ = \ \frac{£24}{6} \ = \ £4 \text{ VAT}$$

This means that the purchase price before VAT was £20 and the VAT was £4.

ratios and fractions

A ratio shows the comparative number of different items in a group.

For example, if you have a class of 22 students which has 9 males and 13 females, the ratio of male to female is 9 to 13; this is written as:

9 : 13

If one of the females dropped out of the class the ratio would become:

9 : 12

Note that you could divide these numbers by the same number, ie 3, to produce the ratio:

3 : 4

It is normal practice to reduce a ratio to the lowest possible whole numbers, by dividing both numbers by the same whole number.

Note also that you can convert a ratio into a fraction. Taking the example of the class where the ratio of males to females is 9 : 13, you can state that:

■ there are 9 males in a group of 22, so the fraction of males in the group is $^9/22$

■ there are 13 females in a group of 22, so the fraction of females in the group is $^{13}/22$

DEALING WITH PERCENTAGES

definition – a percentage is a part of a whole

The phrase 'per cent' means 'out of every hundred'.

So 50% means '50 out of every hundred.' A percentage tells you what proportion one number is in relation to another. In other words, a percentage is a part of a whole, where the whole is 100. It is the top number of a fraction when the bottom number is 100:

$$50\% \quad = \quad \text{the fraction} \quad \frac{50}{100} \quad = \quad \frac{1}{2} \quad \text{ie, a half}$$

If you go to a party where there are twenty people, your partner might use a fraction and say '*I don't know half the people here*'. The way to work out the percentage of people your partner knows is to divide the number known (the 'part') by the total (the 'whole') and then multiply the result of this by 100. The formula is therefore:

$$\frac{\textbf{the part } \textbf{x } \textbf{100}}{\textbf{the whole}} \quad = \quad \textbf{percentage of the part}$$

Suppose your partner knew 12 of the 20 people at the party. The percentage of people known would be:

$$\frac{12 \text{ people } \text{x } 100}{20 \text{ people}} \quad = \quad 60\% \text{ are known}$$

working out a percentage of a given number

This is a very common use of percentages in organisations. Here you **start** with the percentage rate and use it as a number of 'hundredths' to work out the figure you need as a fraction of a given amount. Examples include:

■ **discounts** – an amount to subtract from a money amount

■ **tax** – an amount, VAT for example, to add to sales

This is done by using the formula:

$$\frac{\textbf{given percentage } \textbf{x } \textbf{amount}}{\textbf{100}} \quad = \quad \textbf{percentage amount}$$

Suppose you want to calculate 8% of £250. Using the formula, the calculation is:

$$\frac{8 \text{ (percentage) x } £250 \text{ (amount)}}{100} \quad = \quad £20$$

An easy way of doing this is to shift the decimal place of the percentage figure two places to the left and then put this figure in a calculator and multiply it by the money amount. So in this case 8% becomes 0.08 and the calculation is simply:

$$0.08 \times £250 = £20$$

calculating discount amounts

We will now use the formula explained on the previous page to calculate a discount amount. The invoice extract shown below shows the discount percentage given on the sales transaction. This is most likely to be **trade discount** – ie the discount given to customers who expect a discount as part of the trading relationship.

Calculating discounts involves working out a percentage of the total of the products sold and then **deducting** this from the total. The formula needed to calculate the percentage discount which will be deducted is therefore:

$$\frac{\textbf{sales total (£)} \times \textbf{discount percentage}}{\textbf{100}} = \textbf{discount (£)}$$

Continuing the example on page 75 the sales total is £40 and the trade discount is 20%. Applying the formula, the calculation is:

$$\frac{\text{sales total (£40)} \times \text{discount percentage (20)}}{100} = \text{discount of £8}$$

Note that the discount amount of £8 is not actually shown on the invoice; all you see is the amount before the discount is deducted (£40) and the net amount after the discount is deducted (£32). This may seem confusing, but it is common practice.

product code	description	quantity	price £	unit	total £	discount %	net £
BF-R	Box file (red)	10	4.00	each	40.00	20	32.00

rounding off numbers to decimal places

Sometimes the discount amount will not come out as a precise '£ and pence' figure, ie to two decimal places.

The number of **decimal places** means the quantity of numbers to the right of the decimal point. In money amounts this will obviously always be 2. The calculation may produce something awkward like £91.9324 or £45.5786. In this case the four figures to the right of the decimal point will have to be **rounded up or down** to produce the correct number of decimal places to correspond with the two digits showing pence - ie 2 decimal places. In this case:

£91.93<u>24</u> becomes £91.93 (rounded **down** to the nearest penny)

£45.57<u>86</u> becomes £45.58 (rounded **up** to the nearest penny)

The '**rounding**' rule is therefore:

- start with the right-hand digit of the number
- if it is 5 or higher delete it and add 1 to the digit on its left
- if it is less than 5 delete it and leave the digit on the left as it is
- carry on until you have the right number of decimal places (this is normally 2 decimal places in the case of money amounts in accounting)

rounding to the nearest whole number

When you are told to round a number **to the nearest whole number** look at the number to the right of the decimal point, if it is 5 or greater than 5 the number to the left of the decimal point increases by one, if it is less than five it stays the same.

27.938 rounds to 28 because the 9 tells you to go up

28.345 rounds to 28 because the 3 tells you to stay the same

adding VAT (sales tax) to an invoice

The invoice used in the example on the last few pages is also likely to include Value Added Tax (VAT), which is a sales tax. This is worked out as percentage of the net total after any trade discount has been calculated. Like most taxes, VAT is quoted as a percentage rate, and like most taxes VAT varies from time to time. In this book VAT is quoted at a rate of 20%.

The invoice with the VAT calculation will appear as follows:

product code	description	quantity	price £	unit	total £	discount %	net £
BF-R	Box file (red)	10	4.00	each	40.00	20	32.00
						Total	32.00
						VAT @ 20%	6.40
						TOTAL	38.40

VAT is calculated as a percentage of the cost of the goods. If invoiced goods, as here, cost £32, the VAT (at the standard rate of 20%) is calculated as:

$$\frac{£32 \times 20}{100} = £6.40$$

Important note: if the amount of VAT calculated comes out at more than 2 decimal places, you normally **delete all digits** to the right of the 2 decimal places. This is different from the rounding rule set out at the top of the page.

calculating VAT when it is included in the total

Sometimes you may have to deal with a low value invoice or receipt which quotes a figure which includes VAT at a certain rate, but does not actually tell you what the VAT amount or the cost price is. You may have to calculate this VAT amount and the cost before VAT to enter in the books; for example in the petty cash book.

Let us take an example of a receipt or invoice for £24.00 for some stationery. This includes the cost of the stationery (100%) and also the VAT (20%) added to this cost. The total amount therefore equates to 120% of the cost.

The formula to use in this case is:

$$\frac{\textbf{VAT percentage}}{\textbf{100\% + VAT percentage}} \quad \text{x} \quad \textbf{total amount(£)} \quad = \quad \textbf{VAT content(£)}$$

Applying this formula to the total figure of £24.00, the calculation is:

$$\frac{20\%}{120\%} \quad \text{x} \quad £24.00 \quad = \quad \text{a VAT content of } £4.00$$

Therefore the £24.00 total amount is made up of a cost price of £20.00 and VAT of £4.00 (£20.00 is £24.00 minus £4.00).

If the VAT rate is 20%, another way of working out the VAT included in a total amount is to multiply the whole amount by the **VAT fraction** of $^1/6$, or more simply, divide the whole amount by 6 (see also page 76).

The calculation is therefore £24.00 ÷ 6 = £4.00.

Note that if the VAT rate changes, so will the VAT fraction.

PERCENTAGES FOR MANAGEMENT ACCOUNTING

The application of percentages to your studies so far has concentrated on basic accounting and bookkeeping, using an invoice as an example. Percentages are also very useful for reporting data, comparing the sales and profit results for different periods, for example, or commenting on the extent to which actual sales or profit results compare with the forecast made in a budget. These relate to management accounting (accounting information for decision making by managers).

percentages used for comparison

There are many applications of percentages in management accounting. For example a shop owner might say that:

'60% of our total sales for the year were made in the two months before Christmas.'

This is much clearer than saying:

> *'£240,000 of our annual sales of £400,000 were made in the two months before Christmas.'*

To work out this percentage you need to use the formula:

$$\frac{\textbf{the part of the whole}}{\textbf{the whole}} \quad \textbf{x 100} \quad = \quad \textbf{the percentage}$$

In the example above, the calculation is

$$\frac{£240,000}{£400,000} \quad \text{x 100} \quad = \quad 60\%$$

This is useful, for example, when the business wants to compare pre-Christmas sales with other years:

> *'60% of our sales this year were made in the two months before Christmas; this compares with a figure of 55% for last year.'*

This gives you a much clearer picture than if you said:

> *'£240,000 of our annual sales of £400,000 were made in the two months before Christmas; this compares with £192,500 out of a total of £350,000 made last year.'*

This will only give you a headache.

percentage variances

If you are studying costing you will know that a budget forecast figure may be set as a **target** by an organisation for sales or costs for a future period, for example the next year. When the end of that period is reached the organisation will compare

- the actual results, and
- the target forecast

The difference between the two figures will then be calculated. This difference – the **variance** – is stated by means of an amount which can then be converted to a percentage of the forecast figure. If the percentage is greater than what would be expected, it will need to be reported to management so that action can be taken if necessary.

The example shown below shows a comparison of two years' sales figures for a business which sells modern art pictures. Study the table and read the notes and conclusion that follow.

ART WORLD LIMITED – Annual Sales				
	Forecast £	Actual £	Variance £	Percentage difference from forecast
Year 1	400,000	420,000	+ 20,000	+ 5%
Year 2	420,000	407,400	– 12,600	– 3%

Workings:

■ the first column of figures shows the forecast sales figures

■ the second column of figures shows the actual results for the year

■ the third column shows the variance, ie the difference between the forecast and actual figures (a '+' means more than forecast, a '–' means less than forecast)

■ the last column shows the variance shown as a **percentage of the forecast figure** (not the actual figure); the workings are as follows:

Year 1

$$\frac{\text{Variance (£20,000)} \times 100}{\text{Forecast (£400,000)}} = +5\%$$

Year 2

$$\frac{\text{Variance (– £12,600)} \times 100}{\text{Forecast (£420,000)}} = -3\%$$

Conclusion

1 **Sales for Year 1** are higher than the forecast figure by £20,000.

The percentage difference for Year 1 is + 5%, which means that sales are 5% higher than forecast.

2 **Sales for Year 2** are lower than the forecast figure by £12,600.

The percentage difference for Year 2 is – 3%, which means that sales are 3% lower than forecast.

3 Management will take action if they think it is necessary to do so. They will be happy with the Year 1 where sales are 5% higher than forecast. But in Year 2 they will want to investigate the 3% decrease if the 3% is seen to be significant.

USING AVERAGES

A technique which is useful when reporting on a series of performance figures, such as sales figures, is the use of **averages**. There are three commonly-used types of average: the **mean**, the **median** and the **mode**.

which average?

Suppose the finance manager of a kitchen installation business wanted to know for budgeting purposes the average job completion time in days, from initial enquiry through to final installation. He has just received the figures for the jobs completed last month. The figures are (in days):

20, 25, 35, 35, 35, 36, 37, 55, 60, 65, 65

What is the average job completion time? We will look in turn at the **mean**, **median** and **mode** averages.

the mean

The arithmetic mean is probably the most commonly-used and statistically-reliable form of average. It is also known as a '**weighted average.**'

The arithmetic mean is the sum of all the figures divided by the number of figures.

The sum of 20, 25, 35, 35, 35, 36, 37, 55, 60, 65, 65 = 468

The arithmetic mean $= \dfrac{468}{11} = 42.5$ days

This tells the manager that, on average, a job takes approximately 43 days to complete. This will help him in the planning and budgeting process. **Note:**

- the result is not a whole number of days – rounding up to 43 is necessary
- the result takes into account all values – if there had been an exceptional job taking 165 days instead of 65, the result will have been a mean average of $568 \div 11 = 51.6$ days, a possibly distorted result

the median

The median is the value of the middle figure in a series of figures.

Note that if there is no middle figure, as with an even number of values, the median is the arithmetic mean of the two figures nearest to the middle.

Here the median is 20, 25, 35, 35, 35, **36**, 37, 55, 60, 65, 65 = 36 days.

This will not be as helpful to the manager as the mean in this context; it is useful because it is not distorted by extreme values (eg 185 days) – the mean, however, is more reliable because an equal weighting is given to each value.

the mode

The mode is the value that occurs most often in a series.

In this case the most common period is 35 days (3 jobs), followed closely by 65 days (2 jobs). Note that these two time periods are very widely dispersed. This would suggest that this type of average is not as helpful in the planning process. The mode is more useful in areas such as market research in answering questions such as 'How much do people on average spend on a fast food meal?' or 'What is the most commonly-occurring size of T shirt?'

using the mean in inventory valuation

If you are studying costing you will know that it is important for a business organisation to be able to calculate its inventory value, ie the valuation of all the materials and items it holds. One method of inventory valuation is **AVCO** (short for **AV**erage **CO**st). It is very useful for inventory that is added to from time to time and mixed up with existing inventory.

Take, for example, a business importing and selling Chinese tennis rackets. It buys in its tennis rackets every month and stores them in the warehouse. Because the cost price of the rackets varies each month (due to currency fluctuations) and because the rackets are mixed up with rackets already held in inventory it becomes virtually impossible to value the rackets **unless an average cost is taken**, using the mean (weighted average) method.

The formula for this is:

$$\frac{\textbf{total cost of inventory held}}{\textbf{number of inventory items held}} = \textbf{average cost of an item of inventory}$$

If the total cost of the rackets held is £110,000 (different prices paid for consignments on different invoices over six months) and the number of rackets held is 5,500, the **average cost price** can be worked out as follows:

$$\frac{\textbf{£110,000 (cost of items)}}{\textbf{5,500 (number of items)}} = \textbf{£20 (average cost of item of inventory)}$$

In other words at the time that this calculation was made each racket in the warehouse had cost the business, on average, £20.

The business can then use this figure to work out its selling price and make sure that it makes a profit.

USING TABLES

Tables of figures are often used in accounting and finance for setting out data which is useful to management. Sometimes they can be incorporated into a report (see Chapter 4) to:

■ provide information

■ illustrate a proposal

Figures in a table which covers an extended period of time (eg 'this year' and 'last year') can usefully provide a comparison for sales, costs and profit. The technical term for this type of comparison of numbers over time is **time series analysis**.

Staff working in accounting and finance will need to know how to set out a table so that it is clear and accurate. The most common way of doing this is to use a computer spreadsheet or word processing program. A spreadsheet will also enable graphs and charts to be extracted; these can then be included in a report to illustrate data and trends.

constructing a table

If you are processing a set of figures at work you may have to construct a table; alternatively the table may be in 'pro-forma' form (ready made) or it may be output from a computer information system, be completed as a computer spreadsheet or as a table function in Microsoft Word.

The example shown below shows the sales and profit results for a limited company over a period of four years. Study the table and read the notes that follow.

Amico Ltd: Sales and Profit Statement Report				
	Year 1 £000s	**Year 2** £000s	**Year 3** £000s	**Year 4** £000s
Sales	500	970	1,430	1,912
Net profit	65	95	132	147

■ the title clearly sets out what the data is

■ each time period is shown in a vertical column

■ each time period is clearly headed up (it could be a year, a month or a week)

■ the units for the data are stated below the time period – here £000s are chosen to prevent the table being cluttered up with unnecessary zeros

■ the types of data are set out in two rows and labelled in the left-hand column – ie 'Sales' and 'Net Profit' (which means profit after all expenses have been deducted)

■ lines are added to clarify the table – it is not necessary in this case to draw a line under each row of data as the columns can easily be read across; if, however, there was a large number of columns, lines would be helpful

presenting and interpreting the data

The figures set out in the table on the previous page can be interpreted just by reading them, but a much better picture can be obtained by presenting the data in the form of a graph or chart which will provide a very visual concept of each trend and help the understanding of the report.

This process is often carried out by using a computer spreadsheet (see the section that follows).

USING SPREADSHEETS

what is a spreadsheet?

A spreadsheet can be defined as:

a computer program that organises numbers and text in columns and rows and enables the user to perform numerical calculations

Spreadsheets form part of AAT studies, although at this Foundation level you will not be assessed directly on them or have to construct them. You will however need to know what they are and what they can do.

Spreadsheets are now very widely used by individuals, businesses and other organisations for a variety of purposes:

■ simple and complex calculations

■ presentation of numerical data

■ construction of graphs and charts based on the numerical data

At the top of the next page you can see the basic structure of a spreadsheet. Its main features are as follows:

■ it is set out in rows and columns

■ each column is given a consecutive alphabetic reference, ie A,B,C etc

■ each row is given a consecutive numeric reference, ie 1,2,3,4,5 etc

■ where each column and row intersect is a box known as a 'cell' which is given the reference of the appropriate column and row; in the illustration below cell A2 is highlighted:

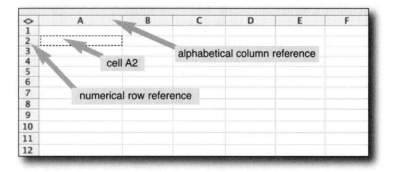

worksheets

Another feature of a spreadsheet file – an Excel file, for example – is the use of worksheets. These are the computer equivalent of separate pages used for calculations in a paper-based system. They are accessed by means of tabs at the bottom of a spreadsheet file, as shown below. In this example it is Worksheet 1 which is being displayed on the screen. Worksheet 2 can be accessed by clicking on the Sheet 2 tab.

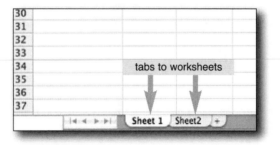

calculations using spreadsheet formulas

One of the major benefits of using spreadsheets in the finance function is its ability to process calculations involving large volumes of numerical data accurately and instantly. In your later AAT studies you will need to be able to set up a spreadsheet using **formulas** for calculations. The main formulas include cell references and symbols, for example:

■ addition: =SUM(B4:B13)

■ subtraction: =SUM(B5-B4)

■ multiplication: =B4*C4

■ division: =B4/C4

To put all this into context, examples of formulas for addition and multiplication are explained and illustrated on the next page.

addition

In order to create a formula you will need to enter an equals sign (=) in the cell which is going to contain the result, followed by the source cell references and symbols needed for the calculation as follows:

■ **simple addition**, use an equals sign followed by the cell references (with numbers) separated by a '+' sign

=B4+B5+B6

■ **addition involving a large number of cells**, eg B4 to B13, use a formula including a ':' symbol:

=SUM(B4:B13)

This is used below to add up a list of sales expenses by sales reps:

◇	A	B	C	D	E	F	G
1	ROPER & CO SALES EXPENSES January - June 20-7						
2							
3	Sales person	Jan	Feb	Mar	Apr	May	Jun
4	Adams	746.00					
5	Duffy	202.50					
6	Fanaletto	233.90					
7	Grundy	67.50					
8	Hanwell	193.60					
9	Marsland	726.12					
10	Pamboris	89.00					
11	Simpson	320.50					
12	Thamiayah	728.50					
13	Wong	973.00					
14	TOTAL	=SUM(B4:B13)					

multiplication

In order to create a multiplication formula, enter an equals sign (=) in the cell which is going to contain the result, followed by the source cell reference, an apostrophe '*' and then the number involved in the multiplication. The left-hand illustration below shows the formula for calculation of sales commission due. The commission rate is 15% of sales and so the number entered in the formula is 0.15, which is the result of 15/100. The formula is therefore:

=B4*0.15

The right-hand illustration below shows the finished result after the formula has been copied into each of the cells in column C.

◇	A	B	C
1	ROPER & CO SALES COMMISSION January 20-7		
2			
3	Sales person	Sales	Commission @ 15%
4	Adams	15060.00	=B4*0.15
5	Duffy	7400.00	
6	Fanaletto	8632.00	
7	Grundy	4529.00	
8	Hanwell	4562.00	
9	Marsland	8481.00	
10	Pamboris	5382.00	

◇	A	B	C
1	ROPER & CO SALES COMMISSION January 20-7		
2			
3	Sales person	Sales	Commission @ 15%
4	Adams	15060.00	2259.00
5	Duffy	7400.00	1110.00
6	Fanaletto	8632.00	1294.80
7	Grundy	4529.00	679.35
8	Hanwell	4562.00	684.30
9	Marsland	8481.00	1272.15
10	Pamboris	5382.00	807.30

spreadsheet graphs and charts

One of the other major advantages of using spreadsheets is that they can create graphs and charts from any selected numerical data. These can be used in reports created and presentations made within the finance function. The examples of charts below give a visual representation of trends and proportions.

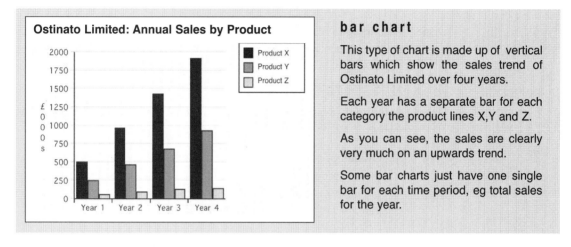

bar chart

This type of chart is made up of vertical bars which show the sales trend of Ostinato Limited over four years.

Each year has a separate bar for each category the product lines X,Y and Z.

As you can see, the sales are clearly very much on an upwards trend.

Some bar charts just have one single bar for each time period, eg total sales for the year.

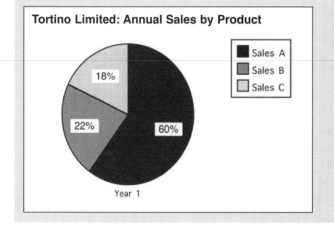

pie chart

This type of chart is circular shaped just like a 'pie'.

Its 'slices' show the proportions of the sales made by Tortino Limited in just one year.

As you can see, the company's most successful product line are is Product A.

Unlike a bar chart this type of chart concentrates on showing proportions rather than any trends.

Reminder: spreadsheets at Foundation level

As noted earlier in this chapter, spreadsheets form part of AAT studies, although at this Foundation level you will not be assessed directly on them or have to construct them or to create charts.

You will however need to know what spreadsheets are and what they can do.

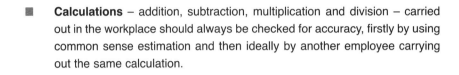

Chapter Summary

- **Calculations** – addition, subtraction, multiplication and division – carried out in the workplace should always be checked for accuracy, firstly by using common sense estimation and then ideally by another employee carrying out the same calculation.

- The principle of **proportion** – the relation of part to a whole – is basic to an understanding of fractions, ratios and percentages.

- **Percentages** are based on the concept of proportion and are commonly used in accounting and finance, for example in the calculation of discounts, Value Added Tax, comparison of performance data, and in budgeting for measuring the difference between actual and forecast figures.

- **Averages** are used in accounting and finance, for example in calculating inventory values in the AVCO (average cost) process.

- The **presentation of numerical data** in table format is an important skill for working in accounting and finance. Tables are often incorporated in reports for management, sometimes supported by graphs and charts which illustrate results and trends very effectively.

- **Spreadsheets** are extremely useful in finance as they can carry out complex calculations accurately and quickly; they can also be set up to produce charts and graphs illustrating trends and proportions.

Key Terms

estimation	using a common sense approach to calculation by seeing if the answer produced seems 'reasonable'
proportion	the numerical relationship between the part to a whole
fraction	two numbers which express the relation of a part to a whole: the top number (the numerator) represents the part and the bottom number (the denominator) represents the whole; an example is $^3/4$ (the part is 3 and the whole is 4)
ratio	the comparative number of different items in a group separated by a colon; an example is 3:4 in a group of 7
percentage	'per cent' means 'out of every hundred,' so a percentage is the part of a whole where the whole is 100; eg if 15 students in a class of 20 have beards the percentage of people with beards as a fraction is $^3/4$, but as in a percentage the bottom number is always 100 the fraction will be $^{75}/100$, ie 75%
decimal place	the number of digits (numbers) to the right of the decimal point; £ and p are quoted to two decimal places, eg £4.99
rounding	in the case of £ and p, reducing the number of digits to two decimal places by rounding up or down to the nearest p

mean average	the sum of a series of figures divided by the number of figures – this is also known as a 'weighted average'
time series	a series of data collected regularly over a period of time, eg annual sales figures
spreadsheet	a computer program that organises numbers and text in columns and rows forming 'cells' into which data is entered enabling the user to perform numerical calculations
worksheet	separate 'pages' of a spreadsheet accessed by tabs at the bottom of the screen
formulas	numbers, cell references and mathematical symbols entered into a spreadsheet cell in order to carry out calculations, the result of which will be shown in that cell
bar chart	a chart which sets out a series of bars, the height of which indicates the extent of the value that varies – useful for illustrating trends
pie chart	a circle divided into sectors to represent in the correct proportion the parts of a whole – like a pie divided into 'slices' which shows the proportions that make up a whole

Activities

5.1 You work in the sales invoice section of Mercury Stationery, a wholesaler. You have a small batch of invoices to process for three different customers. You are required to complete and total the invoice extracts, including trade discount and VAT as required (and rounded down).

(a) 20 box files (black), product code 109BK@ £4.00 each with 30% trade discount

(b) 90 biros (red), product code 235RD @ £5.60 per box of 10, with 20% trade discount

(c) 8 year planners (blue), product code 563BL @ £12.95 each, with 10% trade discount

(a)

Product code	Description	Quantity	Price £	Unit	Total £	Discount %	Net £
						Total	
						VAT @ 20%	
						TOTAL	

(b)

Product code	Description	Quantity	Price £	Unit	Total £	Discount %	Net £
						Total	
						VAT @ 20%	
						TOTAL	

(c)

Product code	Description	Quantity	Price £	Unit	Total £	Discount %	Net £
						Total	
						VAT @ 20%	
						TOTAL	

5.2 You are working out some prices for a customer and note that some discount calculations produce results involving more than 2 decimal places.

You are to use the rounding rules to ensure that all of the following results are reduced to 2 decimal places:

(a) 15% discount on an amount of £45.50

(b) 20% discount on an amount of £44.99

(c) 30% discount on an amount of £21.75

(d) 15% discount on an amount of £390.95

(e) 30% discount on an amount of £964.55

(f) 2.5% discount on an amount of £35.95

5.3 The following amounts include VAT charged at 20%. You are to work out in each case the VAT amount and the amount before VAT was added on.

(a) £49.20

(b) £292.80

(c) £2.28

(d) £436.80

(e) £105.60

5.4   You work for Hypnos Enterprises. You have been asked to complete the following tables showing their annual sales and profit figures for the last two years. You have been asked to calculate and comment on in each case:

(a)   The variance between the forecast and actual figures, noting if it is '+' or '–'

(b)   The variance as a percentage of the forecast figure

HYPNOS ENTERPRISES – Annual Profits				
	Forecast £	Actual £	Variance £	Percentage difference
Year 1	64,000	67,200		
Year 2	65,000	63,050		

HYPNOS ENTERPRISES – Annual Sales				
	Forecast £	Actual £	Variance £	Percentage difference
Year 1	600,000	642,000		
Year 2	640,000	608,000		

5.5   Calculate the average (mean, median and mode) hourly rate of employees' pay from the following figures:

Andy	£7.50
Bella	£7.75
Carlo	£7.80
Dirk	£7.85
Estelle	£7.90
Freddy	£9.00
Gina	£11.00
Hal	£11.00
Ian	£14.20

Which average figure are you likely to use if you are compiling a report on wage costs, and why?

6 Planning and managing your work

this chapter covers...

This chapter explains the need for a person working in an organisation to be able to plan and manage their work in order to help achieve the objectives of the organisation.

The principles set out here apply not just to the finance function but to all areas of the organisation.

An employee must be able to:

■ *work to achieve the objectives of the organisation – for example customer satisfaction and profitability*

■ *work in line with the procedures set out by the organisation*

■ *manage the workload by identifying the different types of task involved*

■ *prioritise these tasks and meet deadlines that have been set*

■ *use appropriate planning aids such as diaries, 'to do' lists, electronic planners, action plans and schedules to help with this process*

■ *understand the importance of communicating clearly and promptly with management and other employees during the completion of tasks and also when deadlines are in danger of not being achieved*

■ *know what to do if things do not go to plan, priorities change and rescheduling becomes necessary*

THE INDIVIDUAL AND THE ORGANISATION

working effectively in finance

It is important that employees learn to treat the workplace as an environment in which they have a sense of responsibility for what they do, for example:

- the everyday tasks that they have to carry out
- working with others to achieve common objectives set by the organisation

'Working effectively' means getting the result that you want. In sport an effective defence prevents the opposing team scoring goals; in the dating game an effective chat-up line could win someone the partner they want. In the workplace an **effective working environment** will result in the achievement of the objectives of the organisation, for example – a motivated workforce, sales and profit targets achieved or exceeded.

Note that 'efficient' is not the same as 'effective'. It means getting the job done with the minimum waste of effort and resources. This is, of course, an important objective in any organisation. But note that an **efficient working environment** will not always be 'effective'. A line manager, for example, may be ruthlessly efficient in saving time and money, but the workforce may be fed up with him or her to the extent that levels of performance will fall off. The working environment will become less 'effective'.

The ideal working environment, therefore, is one that **balances effectiveness and efficiency**. The job is done well with the minimum wastage of effort and resources.

employees and objectives

What are the 'common objectives' of an organisation referred to at the top of this page? They may well include:

- customer satisfaction – making the customer the main focus of the organisation
- profitability – which should benefit employees, owners and customers
- being environmentally friendly – reducing wastage of natural resources, eg energy and paper

In order to achieve these objectives, organisations promote:

- customer care schemes
- profit-sharing schemes
- 'green' schemes to cut down on wastage, eg of energy and paper

These objectives will affect the way in which employees are required to carry out their day-to-day tasks.

The example below shows how a Customer Care scheme used by a financial services company sets very specific targets for the performance of workplace tasks. When an assistant sorts out a customer query, it is not just a case of 'that's another one out of the way' but 'I got a buzz of satisfaction in showing that our organisation cares about its customers.'

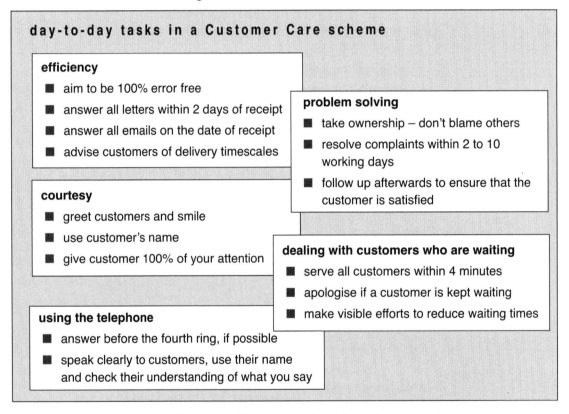

day-to-day tasks in a Customer Care scheme

efficiency
- aim to be 100% error free
- answer all letters within 2 days of receipt
- answer all emails on the date of receipt
- advise customers of delivery timescales

problem solving
- take ownership – don't blame others
- resolve complaints within 2 to 10 working days
- follow up afterwards to ensure that the customer is satisfied

courtesy
- greet customers and smile
- use customer's name
- give customer 100% of your attention

dealing with customers who are waiting
- serve all customers within 4 minutes
- apologise if a customer is kept waiting
- make visible efforts to reduce waiting times

using the telephone
- answer before the fourth ring, if possible
- speak clearly to customers, use their name and check their understanding of what you say

complying with organisational procedures

The way in which employees tackle tasks is often set down in written sets of **procedures**. Larger organisations are likely to have manuals which give guidance; smaller organisations may have written 'checklists' compiled by experienced staff. Examples of tasks in a finance context which will have set procedures for the tasks carried out include:

- checking and paying supplier invoices
- dealing with petty cash
- dealing with cheques and cash being paid into the bank
- processing payroll
- backing up data processed on computer systems

THE NEED TO PRIORITISE TASKS

So far in this chapter we have seen that an employee may have sets of instructions and procedures to learn when doing a job. The day-to-day work will involve a wide variety of tasks competing for the employee's time. These may be **routine** or **non-routine**, **urgent** or **non-urgent**. The employee must develop the skills needed to identify and prioritise the tasks that need to be done. We will now examine the techniques and aids available to the employee to help with this.

keeping to the job description

An employee needs to know:

■ what tasks need to be done in the office

■ what tasks the employee is able to do in the office

These are not necessarily the same. Employees should be given a **job description** which sets out exactly what the employee is expected to be able to do. It may be that a line manager puts pressure onto an employee to carry out tasks which the employee is not qualified or able to do. The employee may think 'promotion here we come!' but also may get in a mess and make mistakes for which he or she should not really be held responsible.

One golden rule is therefore to look at your job description and know what you have to do and what limits there are to your range of activities.

identifying types of tasks

The next golden rule is to be able to identify exactly what tasks have to be done and to identify what type of tasks they are, because this will affect the order in which they are carried out.

There will normally be a number of different types of tasks in a finance office:

■ **routine tasks**

These are everyday tasks such as reading the post and emails, checking invoices, inputting data, sending standard letters and emails, answering telephone queries, photocopying and filing. They may not be particularly challenging, but their efficient completion is important to the smooth running of the office.

■ **non-routine ('ad hoc') tasks**

'Ad hoc' simply means 'for this situation'. These are the unexpected tasks such as helping with one-off projects, working out of the office on a special assignment, or helping to clear up after the washroom has flooded. These may hold up your normal routine work.

Routine tasks are easy to plan for because they are predictable. **Non-routine tasks** cannot be planned for, and they can sometimes cause problems, as we will see later in the chapter.

Tasks may be **urgent** and may be **important**. These are not the same thing:

- **urgent tasks**

  These are tasks which have to be done by a specific pressing deadline: the manager may need a spreadsheet immediately for a meeting currently taking place; customer statements may have to go out in tonight's post.

- **important tasks**

  These are tasks for which you have been given personal responsibility. They may be part of your normal routine and other people depend on their successful completion, or they may have been delegated to you because your line manager thinks you are capable of completing them.

working out the priorities

Prioritising tasks means deciding the order of the tasks. Which one first? Which one last? The two main factors involved in the decision are **urgency** and **importance**. The guide to the basic order of priority is shown below.

an order of priority . . .

1 Tasks that are **urgent and important** – they have got to be done soon and if you do not do them you are going to let a lot of people down – eg producing the spreadsheet for the manager's meeting.

2 Tasks that are **urgent but less important**, eg watering office plants which have dried out – if you fail to water them straightaway the job still needs doing, but the office is not going to grind to a halt if they remain dry.

3 Tasks that are **important but not urgent**, eg producing some sales figures for your line manager for a meeting at the end of the week – the task has to be done, but it could be done tomorrow.

4 Tasks that are **neither important nor urgent**, eg archiving material from some old files. This task is a useful 'filler' when the office becomes less busy; but it would not matter if it were put off for a week or two.

On the next page is a Case Study illustrating these principles. Note in the various situations the importance of the need to **communicate** openly with work colleagues and management when there are problems to be solved.

FLICK'S DAY – WORKING OUT THE PRIORITIES

Flick works as an assistant in the finance office of the Liverpool head office of Estro PLC, a company that makes vacuum cleaners. Her main job is to process incoming sales orders. She is supervised by her line manager Josie Khan.

She is not having a good week and seems stressed by the workload she has been given. It is Thursday 6 February and things are getting no better.

She has written down her tasks on various bits of paper and has stuck post-it notes on the side of her computer screen, marking them 'Remember!' Her colleague, Kirsty, has written notes to her. She also has her daily routine sheet which came with her job description.

These are all shown below.

SALES ORDER PROCESSING: DAILY ROUTINE

1 Collect mail, open, sort and refer where necessary

2 Open email and deal with queries - refer where necessary

3 Check incoming sales orders and debit notes

4 Check sales orders with credit control lists

5 Batch and process sales orders on computer

6 Print sales invoices and credit notes

7 Check printed documents

8 Agree batch total with computer day book summary

9 Pass invoices and credit notes for checking against order documentation

10 File copy invoices, credit notes and order documentation

11 Answer customer queries - refer where necessary

These are the notes received from Kirsty, Flick's colleague:

Flick - Finance Manager wants January sales figures asap!

Kirsty 6 Feb 9.30

Flick - we are moving the computers at 2.00 Thursday afternoon - can you help?
Kirsty

These are the 'Remember!' post-it notes Flick has stuck on the side of her computer screen:

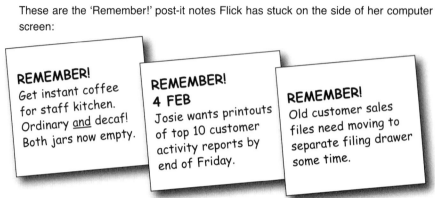

REMEMBER!
Get instant coffee
for staff kitchen.
Ordinary <u>and</u> decaf!
Both jars now empty.

REMEMBER!
4 FEB
Josie wants printouts
of top 10 customer
activity reports by
end of Friday.

REMEMBER!
Old customer sales
files need moving to
separate filing drawer
some time.

How is Flick going to work out her priorities?

solution

Flick takes a short morning break to discuss her various tasks with her line manager, Josie. At Josie's suggestion she thinks about the priorities involved and classifies the tasks according to how urgent they are and how important they are. She starts by prioritising the non-routine/unexpected tasks:

urgent and important tasks

• The Finance Manager wants the January sales figures straightaway.

• The computers have to be moved at 2.00 pm that day.

urgent and less important tasks

• The staff kitchen needs more coffee.

important and non-urgent tasks

• The top 10 customer activity reports are required for Friday.

less important and non-urgent tasks

• The old customer sales files need moving to a separate filing drawer.

The non-routine tasks are fairly easily prioritised, as seen above, although there was some uncertainty over whether the staff coffee or the customer printouts had greater priority! But Flick's problem was how to combine the non-routine tasks with the big pile of routine paperwork she had to get through that day. Then there was the filing to do and customers on the telephone with complicated queries.

Josie, her line manager, suggests that she should deal with her tasks in the following order:

1   urgent and important tasks – the January sales figures, shifting the computers

2   important routine tasks – these include processing and checking documentation, answering customer queries

3   urgent and less important tasks – it will not take long to get some more coffee

4   important and non-urgent tasks – the printouts for the next day (Friday)

5   less important and non-urgent tasks – filing (daily filing and shifting old files)

Josie also suggests that Flick compiles a prioritised 'To Do' list of all her non-routine tasks. She can then tick off the items as she does them. This will replace all the notes and Post-it stickers she has all over her desk. It can also be updated as she is asked to carry out new non-routine tasks.

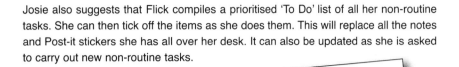

FLICK'S 'TO DO' LIST

1   January sales figures for the Finance Manager.

2   Thursday 2.00 pm move computers.

3   Coffee - get jars of ordinary _and_ decaf at lunch time.

4   Print out top 10 customer activity reports for Josie, Friday.

5   Move old customer sales files to new drawer, as and when.

USING PLANNING AIDS

The Case Study on the last few pages has shown how an employee has become more effective by becoming more organised and prioritising tasks. The Post-it notes are important in the process, but they are only a start. There are a number of planning aids available to help with organisation, time planning and prioritisation in an accounts office. These include:

■ written 'To Do' lists – as seen above

■ diaries

■ calendars and wall planners

■ electronic planners

■ schedules

■ action plans

'To Do' lists

Making lists of things 'to do' is very common both at work and at home, ranging from the type of list shown above to the very basic family shopping list. It is the organised person, however, who writes these lists on an ongoing basis, possibly daily, incorporating actions which have not been ticked off on the previous day in a new list. In other words, tasks that have not been done are carried forward onto a new list. 'To do' lists can be written on paper, or on electronic devices such as work computers.

'To do' lists may be subdivided to show the priorities of the tasks to be done. Look at the example below.

'TO DO' LIST   1 April

urgent stuff

1 Aged debtors schedules for the Finance Manager for today.

2 Sales summaries for Costings section for today.

3 Get March statements in the post today.

non-urgent

1 Print out activity reports for overseas customers.

2 Set up spreadsheet for regional sales analysis.

3 Look into venues for staff evening out.

diaries

The diary organises tasks in terms of time sequence. They are very useful planning aids and ensure – if they are efficiently kept – that tasks and events do not clash. Diaries can be paper-based or electronic. They can be individual diaries or office or 'section' diaries used for a group of employees.

The traditional paper-based diary with a week to view can be used alongside 'To do' lists as an efficient way of time planning and prioritising.

The diary shown below is kept by a line manager.

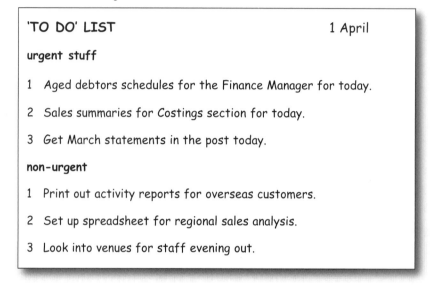

calendars and wall planners

Calendars and wallplanners – often fixed to the wall – are useful visual guides to events and processes taking place in an accounting office, for example:

- ongoing projects, eg installation of a new Sage computer network
- routine activities, eg end-of-month statements, payroll
- staff training, eg work-shadowing and coaching
- and most important of all – holidays

Calendars and wall planners are essentially **team** planning devices.

electronic planning software

The functions of a diary, calendar and prioritisation planner are usefully combined in computer 'planner' software which is available in one form or another on many computers. These provide the functions of:

- a diary
- 'to do' lists
- task prioritisation

The illustration below shows a typical screen from the iCal computer program.

planning schedules

Planning schedules are rather more complex planning devices which deal with situations such as projects where:

■ some tasks *have to* follow on from each other – to give a simple example, you have to boil the water before making a cup of coffee – these are known as **critical** activities; you cannot achieve what you want without doing them in sequence

■ some tasks are **non-critical** – they are important, but the timing is not so crucial – you will have to put coffee in the cup, but you can do it while the kettle is boiling or even at the beginning of the day if you want

So whether you are making coffee or planning a new computer system for the accounting department, the principles remain the same. Organisations often use a visual representation of the tasks in the form of horizontal bars set against a time scale to help with the planning. These can be drawn up manually, or on a computer using dedicated software.

action plans

An **action plan** is a plan which will:

■ define each activity

■ record start and completion dates for individual activities

■ state who is responsible for carrying out each activity

■ in some cases state the cost of each activity

This form of plan is a form of checklist which can be regularly monitored and amended as required. Plans rarely go according 'to plan'. Computer spreadsheets are often used for setting out action plans because they can be easily amended and printed out in revised form. An extract from an action plan is shown below.

marketing action plan

Product 247G - launch date April

Month	Activity	Person in charge	completed	budget £	actual £
Feb	Book press adverts - trade magazines	RP	6 Feb	5,600	5,750
Feb	Leaflet design	HG	12 Feb	1,200	1,200
Feb	Catalogue design	HG	12 Feb	2,400	2,750
March	Leaflet printing	GF		12,000	
March	Catalogue printing	GF		34,500	
March	Press releases	DD		100	
April	Public launch on 1 April	DD		50,000	

DEALING WITH DEADLINES

what to do when you cannot meet deadlines

Things never go quite according to plan. The unexpected can occur and what seems like a quiet productive day can turn into a stressful time, full of awkward decisions. For a finance assistant an important aspect of working is therefore **keeping the line manager advised** of what is going on and communicating any problems that arise. The manager will want to be the first to know. If deadlines are not being met, changes will have to be made:

- tasks may change in order of priority
- tasks may have to be delegated
- tasks may have to be delayed

consequences of poor performance at work

Non-completion or a bad standard of work can have serious consequences. If you work as a finance assistant, or a member of a work 'team' it is important to realise what will happen if:

- work is not completed to the necessary standard
- work is completed late
- work is not completed at all

Not only will the individual feel a failure, but colleagues will be let down and the department will get a bad name. If the public are involved, the reputation of the business may suffer. In these days of online reviews of competitive products and services, a poor review can seriously affect sales.

Here are some examples of how an accounting department could be let down and the reputation of the business affected:

- sales invoices not being checked properly, resulting in customers being overcharged
- statements of account not being sent out which will result in customers not paying their invoices on time and the business becoming short of cash
- careless handling of customer credit card details and the bad publicity which follows if fraudulent transactions result

consequences of good performance at work

If, on the other hand, an employee produces a good standard of work and meets deadlines, this will have a positive effect on colleagues, the team and the whole business. It will also enable the employee to appreciate that his or her contribution to the organisation is valued and important.

The following Case Study describes how a finance assistant faces a number of problems during a working day. It explains how she deals with the problems by communicating with management and colleagues, prioritising and rescheduling her tasks and making a success of the day.

FLICK'S DAY – CHANGING THE PRIORITIES

Flick works as an assistant in the finance office of the Liverpool head office of Estro PLC, a company that makes vacuum cleaners.

The Case Study which starts on page 99 showed how Flick prioritised her tasks on one working day – Thursday 6 February.

In this Case Study we will see how she copes with unexpected events on that day by changing the priorities of her tasks and asking for help from managerial staff where appropriate.

To recap on what Flick had planned for Thursday:

1   The urgent tasks were to provide the January sales figures for the Finance Manager and to help with moving the computers in the afternoon.

2   Flick had planned to get some jars of office coffee at lunchtime.

3   There was the normal daily sales order processing work and filing to be done.

4   Flick also had to provide some customer activity printouts for the following day and had been asked to move some filing records.

Flick's problems

Flick was faced with a number of problems as soon as she got to work on the Thursday. These meant that her carefully thought out work plan was in trouble and would have to be revised. The problems were:

1   **09.30**. Her colleague, Kirsty, who helped her with her sales order processing work had to go home sick. She had eaten a dodgy curry the night before and was in no fit state to work. There was a trainee working on the invoicing as well, but Flick doubted if this trainee could cope with the extra work involved.

2   **10.00**. Flick saw from Kirsty's note that she had to give the Finance Manager the January sales figures 'as soon as possible'. This seemed a bit vague. Did it mean during the morning, or would later in the day be OK?

3   **11.30**. Flick's printer jammed and a long run of invoices was ruined. She could not seem to get it to work again.

4   **12.00**. The Human Resources Manager phoned through to ask if she could 'pop in' to see her at 1.45. Was she free then? Flick knew that she had to move the computers at 2.00.

5   **12.30**. Flick realised that she was going to have to work for most of her lunch break. What about the coffee she was supposed to be getting?

Flick was faced with a number of situations which clearly meant that her work plan was going to be disrupted and would have to be revised. But how was she to do this? She obviously needed to communicate with both management and colleagues about what should be done. Some of the decisions would have to be made by the management.

09.30 Kirsty away off sick

Kirsty's absence would mean that Kirsty's routine processing work would have to be done by someone else – either Flick (who was busy anyway) or the trainee – unless it could be left until the next day. Flick would need to assess how much work there was and then speak to the line manager, Josie. The line manager said to Flick, 'Do what you can, concentrating on orders from the important customers. The rest will have to wait. I don't think the trainee can be left on her own yet'. Flick was not too happy about this because she was very busy herself. She would have to put some of her other tasks back in order of priority.

10.00 the figures for the Finance Manager

Flick realised that this was a priority job. To clarify what 'as soon as possible' really meant, she emailed the Finance Manager who replied that the figures would be needed by lunchtime that day for a meeting in the afternoon. This job remained top priority.

11.30 printer jam

The printer jam had to be referred to the line manager who called in the maintenance engineer. Flick knew that the invoices would have to be printed that day, so she arranged to print them on another printer through the network. She lost valuable time in sorting out this problem and only got back to work at 11.50, by which time she was getting really stressed.

12.00 Human Resources Manager

Flick realised that the 1.45 appointment with the Human Resources Manager would clash with having to move the computers. The request, however, came from a senior manager and took priority over most other tasks. Flick referred the problem to her line manager who said it would be OK for Flick to go to the appointment. Flick was secretly quite pleased to miss lugging the computers about.

12.30 coffee?

Flick realised that she would have to work through some of her lunch hour, which meant that she would not be able to get the coffee. She explained this to Jack, another colleague, who agreed to get the coffee for her.

17.00 end of the day review . . .

Flick is in good spirits because she has had a productive afternoon. Her work targets for the day have largely been completed, despite the changes of plan. The sales figures have been given to the Finance Manager and much of the sales processing work has been completed. Flick has had an interview with the Human Resources Manager and even arranged for the coffee to be bought.

How has this all been achieved? Flick has successfully reworked her priorities and made the most of her resources by using her communication skills, delegating tasks and consulting management where appropriate.

Chapter Summary

■ An individual working independently should be able to combine efficiency and effectiveness when planning the daily workload.

■ Employees working independently should develop the skill of prioritising tasks and be able to plan their activities accordingly.

■ A 'rule of thumb' order of priority for tasks is:

1 urgent and important tasks

2 urgent and less important tasks

3 important and not urgent tasks

4 tasks that are neither urgent nor important

■ Employees should be familiar with different types of planning aids and construct their own 'To Do' lists and diaries and be familiar with electronic planning aids. They should be aware of planning aids such as project planning schedules and action plans, but they will not have to draw them up.

■ Employees should understand the need to monitor the progress of a work plan over time in order to meet deadlines, and have the flexibility to be able to re-prioritise if unexpected events happen.

■ Employees should be able to communicate with management if they need help; they should also be able to delegate tasks if the need arises, maintaining confidentiality where appropriate.

Key Terms		
	effective	getting the result that you want
	efficient	a task done with the minimum of wastage of effort and resources
	non-routine task	an unexpected task which is not part of the everyday work of an employee
	urgent task	a task which has a pressing deadline
	important task	a task which an employee needs to complete and which significantly affects other employees
	'To Do' list	a checklist of tasks, made by an individual, which can be ticked off when they are completed
	schedule	a chart used for planning projects which organises tasks in terms of time and priority
	action plan	a checklist for a series of activities, listing the main tasks, when they have to be done and by whom
	prioritising	planning tasks in order of urgency and importance

Activities

6.1 You work in an accounts office and together with a full-time colleague work on the order processing and invoicing. One morning your colleague telephones in to say that because of a major domestic problem she is unable to come in that day. Your line manager has said that she can have the day off. The colleague has a pile of purchase orders on her desk which need checking before processing and invoicing, but the line manager, who is a bit stressed that morning, has not asked you to do anything about your colleague's work.

Select and tick the most appropriate action to be taken.

(a)	Carry on with your own work and hope that your colleague will come in tomorrow and clear up the backlog	
(b)	Process your colleague's work as quickly as possible before doing your own tasks. This may mean missing out some of the routine checks that are normally made	
(c)	Carry on with your own work until you have the opportunity to refer the problem to your line manager when she is free	
(d)	Refer the problem to the Senior Finance Manager and say that your line manager is too stressed to deal with the problem	

6.2 You will encounter a variety of tasks in an accounts office. They can be classified as follows:

urgent   non-urgent   one-off 'ad hoc'

Complete the following table with the correct classification of task from the above three terms.

Your line manager asks you for the balances of your top 20 customer accounts. She needs the information for a meeting that morning.	
Your line manager asks you to provide information from the office for the accountants who are coming in next week to audit the accounts. You have never done this before as this is normally a senior colleague's responsibility.	
Your colleague reminds you that it is your turn to get the milk from Tesco Express and remarks that the milk has run out.	

6.3   Prioritising tasks involves placing workplace tasks in a specific order. One method of task classification uses the following categories of task:

important but not urgent tasks   **neither important nor urgent tasks**

urgent and important tasks   **urgent but less important tasks**

You are to complete the table below by:

(a)   entering these four categories in the table below in the order in which you would carry them out.

(b)   choosing a reason for the placing of each category of task from the following options:

– sending round a suggestion list for a staff social

– if you don't do this task very soon you are going to let a lot of people down

– setting up a spreadsheet for a meeting in a week's time

– your manager asks you to turn down the heating

Category of task	Choice of task

6.4   There are a number of planning aids that might be found in an accounting office:

action plan   **'to do' list**   **diary**   **wall planner**

Complete the following table with the appropriate planning aid for each situation.

An employee's personal record of tasks and events over a long period of time.	
A detailed plan which involves a number of people and interrelated tasks and events for a specific purpose over a period of time.	
An annual guide which can be used to display staff holidays and external training courses.	
An employee's daily personal record of tasks to be done in the short term.	

Task 6.5

You are a part-time Accounts Assistant employed by Froyd Limited, a printing business. Your main task is to process the payroll, but you also deal with checking incoming payments, preparing payments to suppliers and dealing with petty cash and the petty cash book.

Your working hours are 09.00 to 13.00 Monday to Friday.

You normally attend the weekly staff meeting at 11.00 every Wednesday.

Most employees are salaried and are paid monthly by direct bank transfer (BACS). Their salaries are processed on the last Wednesday of the month and reach their bank account on the last Friday of the month.

Some casual workers have chosen to be paid weekly by BACS and their salaries are processed every Wednesday and reach the bank account every Friday.

Other casual employees are still paid weekly in cash. The payroll for these employees is processed every Wednesday and paid every Friday. One of your jobs is to go to the bank on Thursday to pick up the cash to make up the pay packets for distribution on Friday. At the same time you also pick up from the bank the notes and coins needed to top up the petty cash.

Your normal routine during the week is set out on the schedule below.

Task description	Scheduling of tasks		Time taken
	Day	Time	for task
Process payments received	Monday	9.00	4 hours
Process payments made to suppliers and petty cash payments	Tuesday	9.00	4 hours
Process the payroll (BACS and cash)	Wednesday	9.00	3 hours
Update and balance the petty cash book	Thursday	9.00	2 hour
Visit bank to pick up cash wages and petty cash	Thursday	11.00	1 hour
Lock the cash in the safe and petty cash box	Thursday	12.00	1 hour
Make up cash pay packets and distribute payslips for all employees	Friday	9.00	3 hours

On the last Wednesday in July you and your car are involved in a minor road accident on the way to work. Nobody is hurt but the driver of the other car is not very cooperative and as a result you do not get into the office until 12.00.

The Accounts Manager is very sympathetic as you are a bit shaken up, but he points out that both the weekly and monthly payroll must meet their deadlines as all the staff will need paying on Friday. He suggests that you prioritise what you have to do for the rest of the week. He has agreed to let you work additional hours on Thursday afternoon so that you can ensure that all the tasks are completed.

(a)   Using the table below, write a 'to do' list for the rest of Wednesday morning, Thursday and Friday by listing the tasks in order of completion. Write the task descriptions in the column on the right. Choose from the following tasks:

Make up cash pay packets and distribute payslips for all employees

Update and balance the petty cash book

Deal with payments made to suppliers and petty cash payments

Process the payroll (BACS and cash)

Lock the cash in the safe and petty cash box

Visit the bank to pick up cash wages and petty cash top up

Process payments received

WEDNESDAY/THURSDAY/FRIDAY 'TO DO' LIST (in order of completion)	
Task 1	
Task 2	
Task 3	
Task 4	
Task 5	

(b)   If you **do not** carry out the instructions of the Accounts Manager there might be problems. Indicate below with a tick in the appropriate column whether the following outcomes could have serious consequences for Froyd Ltd or not.

		Serious	**Not serious**
(a)	The staff may not get paid on time		
(b)	The cash from the bank may not get locked away		
(c)	Petty cash reimbursements may be delayed		
(d)	Suppliers may not get paid on time		
(e)	Minor office duties may not get done		

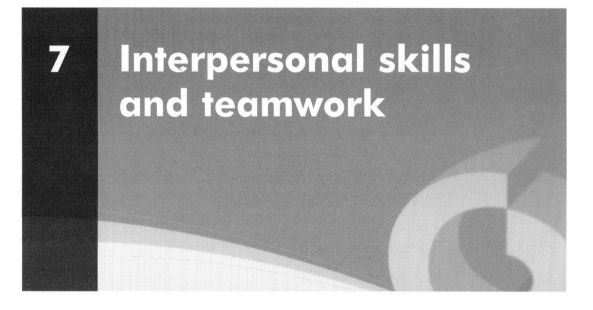

7 Interpersonal skills and teamwork

this chapter covers...

This chapter describes the personal skills which help the workplace to function smoothly and present a professional image of the finance function to customers and other stakeholders. The basic personal skills covered – known as 'interpersonal skills' – include:

- *learning to respect others*
- *learning to communicate and listen to others*
- *developing trust between individuals*
- *being reliable and responsible*
- *developing the skills of negotiation, problem solving and decision making*
- *being professional both with colleagues in the workplace and also in relationships with people outside the business*

Effective teamwork in the workplace also relies on the development of personal skills. Employees working within a team should:

- *identify what they have to do in practical terms to contribute to the work of the team*
- *keep to a plan and the deadlines that have been set*
- *appreciate the consequences to the team and the organisation of not completing tasks that have been set*

This chapter also explains the need for an individual working in an organisation to acquire knowledge and develop professional skills, experience and knowledge in order to:

- *improve himself or herself*
- *meet the needs of the organisation*

A way of achieving this is for the employee, with the help of the employer, to undertake a programme of Continuing Professional Development (CPD).

INTERPERSONAL SKILLS: RESPECT AND TRUST

what are interpersonal skills?

Interpersonal skills are specific 'person-to-person' skills:

- which people develop to enable them to deal with other people within a group
- which ensure that the group functions well and achieves its objectives efficiently and effectively
- which help avoid conflicts of personality and any form of prejudice

In this book these skills are applied to workplace situations, but they are equally important in social and family contexts, as you will know from personal experience!

This first part of this chapter will describe the various personal skills and show how they can improve the performance of a workplace. In each case the explanation of the skills is followed by a summary diagram.

what is respect?

Respect can works in two ways in the workplace:

- you can admire someone else and 'show respect' for their good qualities; for example that person may be very knowledgeable, helpful and a good leader, in which case you will do your best to carry out to the best of your ability the tasks which have been set
- you might be on the receiving end of respect from colleagues who admire – 'have respect' – for your knowledge and experience, in which case you will be motivated to achieve the best possible result for your work team

showing respect

Respect can be shown in a number of different ways, all of which are important in the workplace:

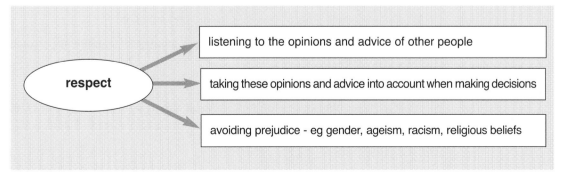

developing trust

When you are working with other people over a period of time it is important that you can rely on their accuracy, honesty and ability to give advice. In other words you can 'trust' them. In a similar way it is equally important that they trust you, which means that the trust becomes mutual.

In the workplace, relations between staff have to be built on trust. A workplace team that has developed mutual trust is an efficient and effective team.

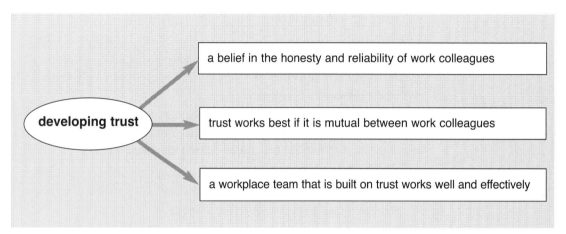

developing trust

a belief in the honesty and reliability of work colleagues

trust works best if it is mutual between work colleagues

a workplace team that is built on trust works well and effectively

THE TWO 'R'S – RELIABILITY AND RESPONSIBILITY

reliability

Being 'reliable' in the workplace means that you have to be trusted so that the tasks you carry out are:

- completed accurately

- completed on time

- communicated where necessary to the relevant people

Reliability can be built up by developing a number of individual personal skills:

- the ability to **multitask**:
  ie have a number of different tasks in progress at different stages of completion at the same time

■ **stress tolerance**:

the ability to keep cool in stressful situations, eg having a manager shouting at you to complete a task more quickly, or working with an uncooperative or uncommunicative colleague

■ **adaptability**:

the ability to switch from one task to another at short notice, or to take on non-routine tasks, eg dealing with an important customer who turns up unexpectedly at the office when no manager is present

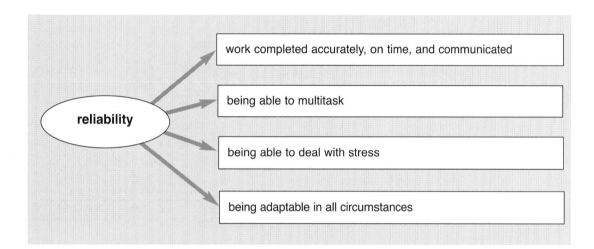

responsibility

A person that is 'responsible' within a workplace is a person who is answerable to the organisation for work which:

■ he or she is completing within a set deadline, or

■ he or she is overseeing, but another employee is carrying out

In other words if the work is not completed on time or satisfactorily 'the buck stops' with the person that is responsible. That person will take the blame for the problem because they can be seen to have ownership of it.

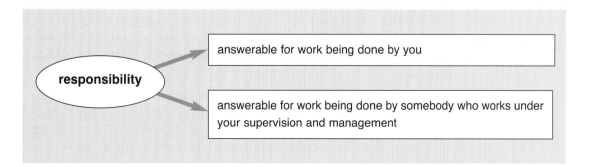

PERSONAL AND LEADERSHIP SKILLS

There are other skills that add to the 'skills set' of a responsible person who acts in any form of supervisory or management role or takes the lead in a workplace situation. These include the following:

inspiring confidence and motivation

If you are taking a leading role in a workplace team or have been appointed to a supervisory role it is important that you should appear positive and encouraging. This will result in the people you work with:

■ gaining **confidence** in what they are doing

■ being **motivated** to work well and successfully complete the tasks they are given; motivation is what pushes them to complete a task when they feel like giving up

showing initiative and problem solving

This involves taking the lead when a problem occurs and working out a successful solution to a problem. The main skills are set out below.

■ **initiative** involves being proactive rather than letting other people take the lead; it means keeping going in the face of setbacks

■ **problem solving** involves having an understanding of all aspects of a situation and coming up with a reasonable and acceptable solution; when problem solving you will need to

– identify the problem, ie what might be wrong

– examine the different options

– act on an agreed course of action

– and lastly, assess its success and whether any changes need to be made

negotiating skills and decision making

It is all part of working in a team and human nature that from time-to-time, team members will disagree about a wide variety of issues. These may range from the type of work they have to do to the temperature setting of the heating in the office. There are two main skills that a team leader or manager will need to resolve these problems: **negotiating skill**s and **decision making**.

■ **negotiating skills** are essential to a team leader; without the use of these skills conflicts within a team may lead to arguments and bad feeling which may result in one or all of the team members feeling dissatisfied. Negotiation involves trying to reach agreements without causing any further dissatisfaction. The essential interpersonal skills required for negotiation are:

– effective verbal communication

– listening skills

– showing consideration and respect for all team members

– problem solving

– and lastly and importantly, decision making

■ **decision making** is the process of making a choice between various alternatives; it is a skill employed by everyone every day, it could involve deciding on the type of pizza you want for tea or it might be the course of action taken at the end of a difficult negotiation process in the workplace.

If you are taking a leading role in a team, the decision making should involve the following processes:

– making sure you know exactly what the problem is and that you are aware of the alternative solutions

– investigating those possible solutions in detail in consultation with the team

– making the decision

– communicating the decision to the team members and ensuring that any team member who is not happy with the decision is given a full explanation and justification of what has been decided.

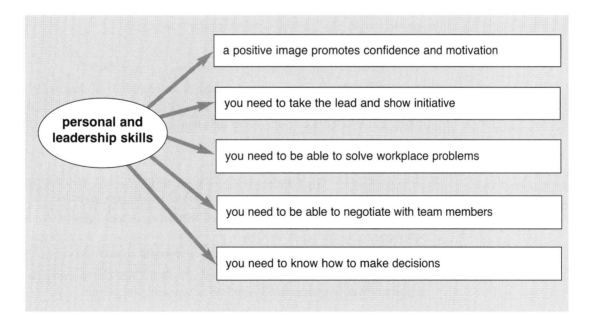

A PROFESSIONAL IMAGE FOR BUSINESS RELATIONSHIPS

a professional image

The success and popularity of a business is often the result of the professionalism of its employees. Customers like dealing with efficient and welcoming staff, and employees enjoy working in a professional and supportive environment.

Being 'professional' in the workplace means using all the skills and appropriate knowledge expected of skilled and trained people in that occupation. Professionalism is important in all organisations. Whether you are working as a partner in an accountancy firm or serving behind a bar, the same principles apply. These professional skills include:

- personal skills, eg communication, politeness, appearance
- skills associated with the business itself, eg product knowledge, awareness of regulations applicable to products and procedures

If you are giving tax advice as an accountant or serving an alcoholic drink at a bar, your professionalism will involve being polite to the customer and knowing what you are doing. You will need to look presentable and know your product. In the case of the accountant you will need to know about the Finance Acts, and in the case of the bartender you will need to know the licencing regulations (eg age limits for alcohol sales or serving hours).

being professional

Listed below are some of the skills associated with 'being professional' as described above. They can be divided into two categories:

- making an impression
- skills needed for building a long-term business relationship

In the skills shown here the example given is an employee dealing with a customer; the skills would equally apply when dealing with a supplier, bank manager, the VAT Office or any other stakeholder.

making impressions

- making a **personal impact** when meeting, speaking to a customer or sending an email: appearing positive, confident and knowledgeable
- **looking good** - if you meet a customer face-to-face, look smart in your appearance by taking care of what you wear and how you do your hair, give eye contact (but do not overdo it as you might appear scary)
- **speak clearly** - choose your words carefully, do not use jargon which the customer will not understand – and do not mumble or gabble

- **listen carefully** and allow customers to say what they want to say

- always **be polite** in face-to-face situations and written communications, never using swear words and bad language, even if the customer does

- uses **business language** and terminology where appropriate (but avoiding jargon) in face-to-face situations and written communications – for example avoid the temptation to use 'text speak' in emails

- when meeting a customer face-to-face:

  - ensure your working environment is clean, tidy and well presented

  - make sure you use appropriate body language and appear interested and helpful

These last two points are illustrated in the two contrasting pictures below.

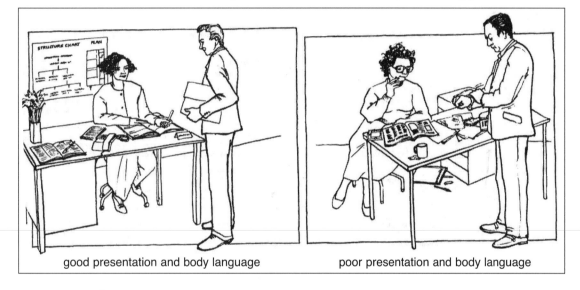

good presentation and body language

poor presentation and body language

maintaining business relationships

A business which projects a professional image through its employees is more likely to build up a longer lasting relationship with its customers. Projecting a professional image will encourage customer loyalty and sales, which in turn will improve the profitability and sustainability of the business.

A business must also take care that it does not spoil this relationship by actions which could breach **ethical rules** of behaviour, for example:

- it must deal **honestly**: it must not give misleading product descriptions

- it must deal with **integrity**, for example:

  - it must not give preferential treatment (eg a larger than normal discount) to a customer who may be a personal friend

  - it should not allow a customer to buy an expensive product which is clearly unsuitable for the customer's requirements

TEAMWORK

what is a team?

Working with others implies the need for teamwork. It is easy to start to define a team by giving examples – a football team, a workplace team – and explaining that they work together – sometimes well and sometimes not quite so well.

But what exactly is a team?

A team is a group of people working together to achieve defined objectives in an effective way.

In the finance function a team is usually a department or 'section' working in a specific part of an office – eg a payroll section or a sales ledger section. The objective of this 'team' will be to complete the required work:

■ to a **high standard**

■ within the required **deadlines**

■ **efficiently** – not wasting any effort or resources

■ **effectively** – achieving the objectives of the tasks that have been set (eg issuing all customer statements by the end of the month)

the characteristics of an effective team

An effective team should ideally have:

■ a **team leader** who is experienced, respected and who motivates the team

■ a shared **common purpose**

■ **motivation** – people get a 'buzz' out of working in a team – it gets people going and brings its rewards when the team is successful

■ clearly defined **roles and responsibilities**

■ good **channels of communication**

■ **shared values** – ie a common motivation to work well and as part of a team

■ **pooling of complementary skills and abilities** – some people are better at some tasks and some are better at others, and so a team will take advantage of individual strengths and overcome individual weaknesses

■ **creative thinking** – working with other people means that individuals can be stimulated to create and share ideas on a scale that would probably not be possible if they were working on their own

■ **help and support** – team members usually support each other when support is needed – this can take the form of advice, moral support and assisting with or taking over tasks which may be causing a problem

teamwork

Teamwork requires each member to be dedicated to achieving the team objectives. Team members in an effective team which performs well should:

■ be committed to the work of the team

■ share the team's values

■ share the team's goals

■ have complete trust in the other members of the team

■ understand their role in the team and the tasks they are allotted

■ be fully aware of their responsibilities and have full ownership for what they do

■ assume joint responsibility for the work of the whole team

■ take note of and work to the schedules established by the team

ideal qualities of a team member

In order to create good working relationships, as a team member you should ideally:

■ be pleasant and polite to other team members

■ be prepared to cooperate, even if you do not agree with everything that is decided

■ respect the opinions of others and be prepared to listen to what they have to say so that they feel that their contribution is valued

■ ask others if you need help and be prepared to help others if they need it

■ avoid backbiting and criticising the leader behind his/her back

the importance of meeting deadlines

The finance function is normally set up in a way that nobody works on their own, and so the non-completion of tasks can have serious consequences for the team and ultimately for the organisation itself.

As we saw in the last chapter, it is important for the individual to plan out tasks that have to be done and the time that it will take to complete them. This also has to be done to ensure that the team runs smoothly and the organisation is seen to be efficient by its customers.

what can go wrong?

In an ideal team nothing will go wrong. You are likely to know from experience that ideal teams are very rare and that things do go wrong within most teams. That's life.

The following Case Study shows what can go wrong in a finance office and how the mistakes made by one member of staff can potentially affect the reputation of the office both within the business and also with customers.

It also shows how the situation can be resolved through effective team management and support for someone who lacks experience and confidence.

Case Study

GINA – WHAT HAPPENS WHEN YOU MAKE MISTAKES

Gina Cavolata is a new addition to the finance team. She has worked in a finance office before and is studying for her AAT Foundation Level exams.

In her first week she has made two mistakes which could have consequences for the reputation of the team and the business. Her manager calls her in to discuss what has gone wrong and how it all reflects on the team.

mistake 1 - a forgotten request for sales figures

The Sales Manager has asked the Finance Department for a breakdown of the last six months' sales figures for a meeting he is having the following day with an important customer. He wants the figures as soon as possible and by the end of the day at the latest. Gina is asked to extract the figures. She writes herself a note to remind herself to print out the figures on a spreadsheet but as she is stressed she forgets all about it. At the end of the day the Sales Manager phones the Finance Manager to ask why there is a delay. He is not very happy. Gina is asked to stay late to produce the figures.

mistake 2 - an incorrect discount on a sales invoice

Gina is asked to help out with the invoicing of sales orders. She issues one invoice to H A Vock Ltd with a trade discount of 20% deducted instead of the 25% normally allowed to this customer. The mistake is picked up by the Accounts Assistant checking the invoice and brought to the attention of the Finance Manager.

Gina's interview

Gina is a new recruit to the business and the manager is concerned about her lack of organisational skills and her ability to handle numbers. The manager does however realise that Gina has only just started her new job and so lacks confidence and experience.

The manager realises that Gina will need a lot of support and so gives her a gentle one-to-one session about the need for her to develop her business skills, explaining how mistakes can refect on the Finance Team as a whole and also potentially affect dealings with customers.

The manager points out:

"Just think what would have happened if the Finance Team had not picked up your mistakes.

In the case of the sales figures not being provided as requested the Finance Team would be made to look inefficient to the Sales Manager. Also if the Sales Manager had not been given the information he would have looked unprofessional in the eyes of the customer whom he was meeting the next day. That would not have reflected well on the business.

In the case of the invoice with the incorrect discount deducted, if it had been sent out to the customer it would not have reflected well on your Finance Team colleagues or on me. The customer is likely to have complained to the Finance Team so that both I, the team and the business itself would have looked unprofessional."

But the manager wishes to be constructive in her advice and finishes by saying to Gina:

"I suggest that you:

– organise your tasks so that you do not forget anything; keeping and updating a 'to do' list on a regular basis is a good start (ask a colleague to show you how to do this if you need help)

– talk to your colleagues if you are unsure about our checking systems and our discount schedules; if in doubt consult our Procedures Manuals

– remember that the standards to which you work can reflect both on yourself, the Finance Team as a whole and potentially the whole business when customers are involved

Lastly – we are here to support you. If in doubt about anything, just ask. Don't get stressed. If you feel unsure about the work we can always arrange for you to work alongside one of your colleagues. I am sure you will soon become an excellent Team member and enjoy working here."

the role of the manager

As you will see from this Case Study the role of the manager is important in running and maintaining an effective team. It is better for the manager to suggest solutions rather than to criticise team members in a harsh manner. Being positive will motivate employees but being completely negative may well have the opposite effect. In the next section you will see that the role of the manager is also important in developing the professional development of the employees.

CONTINUING PROFESSIONAL DEVELOPMENT (CPD)

what is CPD?

Continuing Professional Development (CPD) can be defined as:

the learning activities undertaken by employees to maintain, improve and broaden the knowledge and skills required in their professional lives.

Continuing Professional Development (CPD) is an ongoing cycle – a process involving both employee and employer. It is normally up to the employee to complete the planned activities in order to achieve the level of professional competence required by the professional body to which he or she belongs.

reviewing your performance so far

In order to improve performance and career prospects in the finance function you need to take stock of your current position and then identify exactly what you want to achieve and what it is you need to do to get there. The main stages in this process are therefore:

1   identifying your development needs

2   identifying objectives, ie what you need to do

3   planning how those objectives can be achieved

This process is often formalised during a staff appraisal with a manager who is in a position to provide the necessary guidance and to help make the necessary arrangements.

defining your objectives

Your objectives – targets – for achievement should not be vague and woolly like 'I want to be a manager' or 'I want to be better at my work' but will be very specific. For example you might say that within the next twelve months:

'I need to learn more about spreadsheets because they are used a lot in the Finance Department.'

'I need to learn more about the Sage computer accounting system. I can do the basics, but haven't a clue about doing journal entries.'

'I'd like to do an accounting qualification – it should help me to get on in my career.'

achieving your objectives

These objectives may be met through a variety of planned activities, for example:

- ■ **on-the-job training** – being taught by a colleague, working alongside a colleague (work shadowing), attending formal in-house courses, following 'tutorials' provided online or with software used in the office

- ■ **external training courses** run by your organisation (if it has a separate training centre) or by an independent training body – for example a Health & Safety course or Excel spreadsheet course run by the local Chamber of Commerce or College

- ■ taking **qualifications** such as an AAT Accounting qualification – studying at a local college or with a distance learning provider

The important point here is that you cannot expect to do everything at once. You will need to sit down with your manager and work out a suitable and realistic programme which can be followed and then reviewed after a set period of time.

assessing your success and moving ahead

The process of personal planning never stands still. As in any planning process, achievement will have to be monitored on a regular basis, for example at the annual appraisal interview when both the employer and the employee will need to re-assess the situation. The planning process can then start all over again – new objectives, new targets, a new action plan.

In the Case Study which follows we look at the personal planning carried out by a typical accounting employee.

Case Study

CPD – MAKING THE MOST OF YOUR RESOURCES

situation

Kelly works in the Finance Department of CompLink Limited, a computer supplies wholesaler. She moves to some extent between the sections, but spends most of her time in Sales Ledger, where she processes sales orders on the computer accounting system, checks documentation and has started basic work in Credit Control, sending out statements to customers.

Kelly wants to get on in her job and career. At her appraisal interview in July, she agreed with her manager that she should achieve certain targets within the next twelve months as part of her Continuing Professional Development.

These objectives included:

- in-house training in credit control procedures in the Finance Department, achieved by work-shadowing (working alongside a senior colleague in Credit Control)

- attending an intensive two day training course in computer accounting at a local external training provider

- enrolment at the local college to take an AAT Foundation Accounting course, which runs from September to the following June

solution

Kelly makes good use of the various resources available to help her in her CPD:

colleagues

Kelly can talk to her colleagues and make the most of their experience and knowledge, picking up tips about dealing with procedures and situations. This is particularly useful in Credit Control where Kelly can learn how to deal with slow payers – interpreting all their lame excuses about not paying (eg 'payment has been authorised but has not yet been put through the system' or 'we don't seem to have received the invoice'). She will also learn how to send out the appropriate chaser letters without offending the 'important' customers who sometimes pay late.

training provider

Studying accounting at a local college is never an easy option, but Kelly finds that having a good teacher and a lively class helps her understand the more difficult areas of the course. She is able to ask questions about the areas she finds difficult and is given help when her trial balance doesn't balance.

textbooks

Kelly uses the Osborne Books range of accounting texts and finds that they help her understand difficult concepts and prepare her well for assessments. She is online at home and finds the resources on the publisher's website (www.osbornebooks.co.uk) a big help. She has also invested in the Osborne Books pocket-sized 'Wise Guides' which are very handy for revision.

other websites

The websites of accounting bodies such as AAT are full of useful information and links. The site www.aat.org.uk provides Student Forums and offers e-learning opportunities.

Kelly also uses the website of HM Revenue & Customs (www.HMRC.gov.uk) to answer queries about VAT which have cropped up at work.

and finally . . .

At the end of the twelve months Kelly discusses with her manager the extent to which she has been successful in achieving her objectives:

- Following her in-house training and work-shadowing she is now able to operate the customer debt chasing system without supervision.

- She completed her computer accounting course successfully and has been able to take on more advanced input work.

- She passed all her accounting exams.

She is now in a position to set the objectives for the next twelve months. For example she may have further in-house training, go on a computer spreadsheet course, and take the next stage of her accounting qualification.

Chapter Summary

■ Interpersonal skills help the workplace to function smoothly and present a professional image of the finance team and finance function to customers and other stakeholders. These skills include:

– respecting others

– communicating and listening to others

– developing trust in the workplace

– being reliable and responsible

– being able to negotiate, solve problems and make decisions

– being professional with colleagues and in business relationships with people outside the business

■ Effective teamwork is needed if a group of employees is to achieve its objectives.

■ Members of a team should be able to complete work accurately and on time.

■ An effective team should ideally include:

– an effective leader

– excellent communication between colleagues

– a combination of complementary skills

– shared values and common objectives

■ The team should present a consistently professional image within the group, to other areas of the business and to outsiders such as customers.

■ Unprofessional behaviour reflects badly on the team member, the team and ultimately the business.

■ Improving performance through Continuing Professional Development (CPD) involves a number of stages, starting with an assessment of current knowledge, skills and experience and the need for further training and study.

■ Defined objectives and associated activities can be planned and defined – often in an appraisal interview.

■ An employee should then work out how he or she is going to achieve these objectives, assessing the resources that are going to be needed. These could include tapping into the expertise of colleagues, training in-house, taking a qualification, obtaining study material in various media.

■ The final stage in the personal development process is to review and evaluate progress and to establish new targets and action plans. This may be carried out with the employer as part of the regular appraisal process.

Key Terms		
	interpersonal skills	skills that people develop to enable them to interact effectively with other members of a group
	respect	admiring someone else for their knowledge and experience
	trust	relying on someone else for their honesty, capability and reliability
	reliability	being trusted for accuracy, keeping to time schedules and communicating to others when necessary
	responsibility	being answerable for work done by you or by someone who is answerable to you
	decision making	the process of making a choice between various alternatives
	negotiation	aiming to reach agreement between team members without causing any dissatisfaction
	problem solving	having an understanding of all aspects of a situation and coming up with a reasonable and acceptable solution
	professional	being professional in the workplace means using the skills and having the knowledge of skilled and trained people normally employed in that area of work
	team	a group of people working together to achieve defined objectives
	teamwork	the need for each team member to be dedicated to achieving the team's objectives
	CPD	Continuing Professional Development (CPD) involves an agreed set of learning activities undertaken by employees to maintain, improve and broaden the knowledge and skills required in their professional lives
	objectives	targets for development needs
	knowledge	what an employee needs to know to be able to work effectively
	skills	the ability to put knowledge into practice
	appraisal	the process whereby a manager interviews an employee on a regular basis, assessing past performance and identifying development needs
	performance	the success rate in achieving development needs

Activities

7.1   Important interpersonal skills include the following:

communicating effectively

respecting others

developing trust

being reliable

being responsible

presenting a professional image

You are to read the situations described in the left-hand column in the table below. Then enter in the right-hand column the interpersonal skill that applies to that situation.

Situation	Interpersonal skill
(a) Admiring a colleague who is able to process sales invoices quickly and accurately	
(b) Learning that a particular colleague will give the correct answer to a question	
(c) A colleague who will always get a task done on time and with no mistakes	
(d) A colleague who gives you instructions which you can easily follow	
(e) A colleague who always dresses smartly and deals with customers politely	
(f) A colleague who is in charge of the computer input staff and answerable for what they do	

7.2 Which **one** of the following is the most accurate definition of an employee who can be said to be 'professional'. Select the correct option.

(a) Wearing the smartest clothes and speaking more than one language	
(b) Someone who has a degree in Business Management	
(c) Using the skills and having the knowledge expected of their occupation	
(d) Someone who is a manager or supervisor in charge of other employees	

7.3 Which **one** of the following is the most appropriate form of body language to be used by an employee in a business dealing with a customer who buys from the business. Select the correct option.

(a) Always looking in the customer's eyes	
(b) Never looking in the customer's eyes	
(c) Welcoming and shaking hands with the customer	
(d) Welcoming and giving the customer a big hug	

7.4 Select from the list below **three** characteristics of an effective team.

(a) Members compete to finish their tasks as quickly as possible	
(b) Members understand their role in the team and what they have to do	
(c) Members are prepared to carry out tasks for other members if necessary	
(d) Members must all be professionally qualified to the same level	
(e) Members must maintain good levels of communication with each other	

7.5 You work as an assistant in a Finance Department. A new assistant who has recently been transferred from another section has been given a desk next to you. He spends a lot of work time texting on his mobile phone and so is not completing his purchase invoicing work on time, and when he does complete it he sometimes makes mistakes. The Department is not very busy at the moment.

What effect could this behaviour have on the business? Select the **one** appropriate option.

(a)	No effect because the Department is not busy at the moment	
(b)	It would reflect badly on him because of his behaviour	
(c)	It would reflect badly on the Department and also the business because suppliers may not get paid on time and errors occur	

7.6 Refer to the situation set out in 7.5 above and decide from the actions suggested below what action you would take to resolve the problem? Select **one** option.

(a)	Do nothing at all because you can help him and check his work for him	
(b)	Mention the problem to your line manager if the situation does not improve	
(c)	Mention the problem to the Finance Director	

7.7 The four stages in the CPD process are set out below on the left. You are to match them with the four statements which are set out on the right. Draw lines linking the appropriate statements with the four stages.

Stages

Identifying needs

Setting objectives

Achieving objectives

Evaluation

Statements

Passed the Foundation Level exams

Examining weaknesses in knowledge and skills

Deciding to go on a spreadsheet course

Discussing achievement of objectives with the line manager

8 Ethics, sustainability and Corporate Social Responsibility

this chapter covers...

This chapter covers three areas which affect both employers and employees working in business: ethics, sustainability and Corporate Social Responsibility:

■ **Ethics** in the workplace involves knowing about and practising basic principles of good and acceptable behaviour at work:

– acting with honesty and fairness

– behaving in a professional way and developing professional knowledge

– maintaining confidentiality

■ **Sustainability** is a general term which is used a great deal nowadays to cover a wide range of activities which benefit employees, society and the environment, for example:

– making a profit which benefits society by providing work opportunities

– energy conservation (eg cycle to work schemes, car sharing)

– recycling of waste and other materials (eg paper, plastics)

– helping the community (eg sports sponsorship, charity events)

■ **Corporate Social Responsibility (CSR)** is a very specific term which describes the various policies adopted by an individual business to put the principles of sustainability into practice.

ETHICS IN THE WORKPLACE

a definition

Ethics in the workplace can be defined as:

'the moral principles or standards that govern the conduct of the members of an organisation'.

In other words, ethics affect the way in which employees should behave, both in the workplace and when representing their organisation outside the workplace. As you will see from this, employees do not 'switch off' ethical behaviour when they leave work. Not only do they have to behave in an ethical way in a Finance Department, they have to have the interests of the organisation in mind when at home talking to the family and when out socially with friends who may happen to have a commercial interest in the organisation, for example as a customer or as a supplier.

ethical principles

Many professions – including the accounting profession (and AAT) – have their own written Code of Ethics. These are all based on **fundamental ethical principles**, which are the rules that guide ethical behaviour.

You do not need to know the names and details of these principles at this level of study, as you will study them in detail at higher levels. In this chapter all you need to know is the way ethical behaviour works in practice, concentrating on the three main areas of ethics:

- honesty and fairness
- acting in a professional way
- maintaining confidentiality

We will illustrate these three main areas by providing a number of practical examples which will relate specifically to the finance function in the workplace.

honesty and fairness

Employees in a finance function should:

- be **straightforward** – they should respect and obey rules and procedures
- be **honest** – they should not cover up the truth, fiddle the books, or allow anything to pass through the accounting system which they know has not been checked

■ be **truthful** – they should not tell lies, falsify or 'fudge' figures, or mislead customers and suppliers with false information, eg prices, discounts

■ practise **fair dealing** – they should treat everyone (eg customers and suppliers) on an equal basis

Also, an employee should **not**:

■ get involved in a **conflict of interest** – a situation where professional judgement is affected because the employee could benefit personally from a transaction

■ get involved in a situation where someone is putting **undue influence** on an employee to do something that is dishonest and 'against the rules'

Here are some examples of unethical behaviour:

not being honest or fair

1 A Finance Manager takes his wife on a holiday trip to Paris and charges the expenses to his employer.
Verdict: he is not honest

2 An Accounts Assistant buys herself and some friends some sandwiches and coffee at the local Costa cafe and uses the receipt to reclaim the money from petty cash, stating that it was an expense for 'entertaining customers'.
Verdict: she is not honest or truthful

3 An Accounts Manager lets a customer pay invoices late because the customer is his next-door neighbour and he owes him a favour.
Verdict: this a case of conflict of interest

4 A Finance Manager promises to recommend an assistant for promotion if the assistant keeps quiet about the fact that he has found out that the Manager takes his wife to Paris on company expenses.
Verdict: the Manager is exerting undue influence over the assistant

acting in a professional way

We saw in the last Chapter (pages 120-121) that being professional means 'using all the skills and appropriate knowledge expected of skilled and trained people in that profession'. In terms of workplace ethics, being 'professional' involves **professional competence** and **due care**.

Professional competence means achieving a level of knowledge and skills needed for working at a particular level in the workplace – the more senior the employee, the greater the knowledge and skills that will be needed.

Due care means that the employee must take the required level of care appropriate to the task that is being done. In other words an employee in a finance function must provide a competent and 'professional' service.

Professional competence and due care requires that an employee should:

■ act **professionally** – this means carrying out a task according to instructions, carefully, thoroughly and on time

■ use **sound judgement** in applying professional knowledge

■ know when to **refuse to carry out an area of work** (eg payroll processing) if the employee does not have the necessary knowledge or skills

■ plan career progression through **CPD** (**Continuing Professional Development**), a programme of qualifications, internal courses and expanding experience

Here are some examples of the wrong type of behaviour:

breaches of professional competence and due care

1 A Finance line manager has been asked to take responsibility for the Payroll Section for a few months to cover maternity leave. She has no real experience of this area of the accounting system, but agrees to the request because she is looking for promotion.

Verdict: the line manager is not taking notice of the requirement for professional competence – she may not know what she is doing.

2 A Finance Assistant needs to prepare a spreadsheet showing up-to-date financial figures for the Finance Manager who is attending a company Board Meeting on the following day.

He is in a hurry to get off to meet his girlfriend after work and fails to check the figures he has input, some of which he has accidentally picked up from the previous financial year. He assumes they will be correct and says to a colleague 'this data should be OK because the spreadsheet is always accurate in its calculations'.

Verdict: the Finance Assistant is not taking due care in his professional duties. He has made mistakes which could create trouble for the manager.

confidentiality

Confidentiality is the duty not to disclose information held by the business about another person or organisation to anyone else, unless permission has been given by that person or organisation.

The type of information that should not be given to outsiders includes personal or business details of:

■ customers and clients

■ suppliers

■ colleagues

■ internal information about the organisation

'Outsiders' who should not be given information include:

■ family members

■ social acquaintances

■ 'cold callers', eg marketing survey companies

Here are some examples of incorrect behaviour by employees in the finance function.

breaches of confidentiality

1 A customer telephones and asks a newly-appointed accounts assistant what rate of trade discount another customer receives. The accounts assistant looks it up and tells the customer on the phone that it is 35%.

   Verdict: the accounts assistant has breached confidentiality in giving out details of another customer.

2 A man contacts a business and speaks to a finance assistant. The man wants the mobile number of the finance assistant's colleague. He says that the matter is urgent and he is a good friend of the colleague. The finance assistant looks on his mobile and gives him the number.

   Verdict: the accounts assistant has breached confidentiality in giving out details of a colleague.

3 A sales ledger assistant asks a payroll assistant (a good friend) what the salary of the sales ledger line manager is, as she too wants to become a line manager. The payroll assistant agrees to look it up in the payroll system and gives her the information.

   Verdict: the payroll assistant has breached confidentiality in giving out internal confidential information.

confidentiality – the Data Protection Act

The **Data Protection Act** is the UK law which protects **personal data** from being released to outsiders and makes it an offence to release this information without permission from the person whose data it is. The Act covers:

■ data about individuals (eg sole traders) but **not** about limited companies

■ records held on computer – eg a computer database of names, addresses, telephone numbers, sales details of each customer

■ manual records – ie paper documents, eg statements, letters

The Act states that the data held must be accurate, kept securely and made available on request to the person whose data is held on file. The person is likely to have to pay a small fee for this service.

situations where information can be disclosed

If there were no exceptions to the confidentiality rule, the transfer of information could become a problem, so the person or organisation whose information is involved can give **consent** for the release of the information. Accountants, for example, will obtain permission from clients to release financial information to third parties.

Also note that:

■ there is a **legal duty** to disclose information, eg if an employee suspects a client is involved in money laundering, ie transferring money received from criminal activity into an apparently legitimate account and so changing 'bad' money into 'good' money

■ in some cases the disclosure is in the **public interest**, eg a client who appears to be involved in or funding terrorist activities

Here are some examples of these types of situation:

---

deciding if personal information can be disclosed

1 An accountancy firm doing an audit notices that the client is regularly receiving large sums of money from undocumented sources and is then transferring them into an overseas savings account.

Verdict: the client appears to be laundering the funds and so the accountancy firm will need to disclose this information to the authorities.

2 Sid is a sole trader attempting to set up a credit card account in his name, but the request is refused. Sid asks the credit card company if he can see if there is anything in his credit history which is blocking the application.

Verdict: the Data Protection Act states that he is entitled to see his credit history on request and payment of a fee.

SUSTAINABILITY

sustainability – the three pillars

'**Sustainability**' is a term that describes the need for organisations and individuals to become 'green' and adopt policies which protect the environment, save energy and benefit society as a whole.

The three main objectives of sustainability, known as the 'three pillars of sustainability' are:

- economic growth

- environmental protection

- social equality

These are sometimes also referred to as 'profit, planet and people' – which is a useful way of remembering the three main objectives.

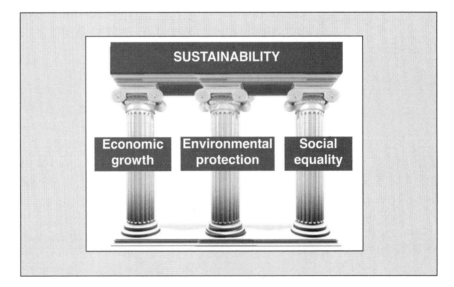

economic growth

Economic growth is important because it makes sustainable development possible. The term 'economic growth' relates to the making of profit by organisations that will bring financial benefits to owners, employees and to the economy locally and nationally.

Examples of the benefits of economic growth include:

- using company profits to make donations to national charities
- using company profits to support events in the local community

environmental protection

The need to protect the environment and conserve resources – the 'green' factor – is one that is most commonly associated with sustainability. Examples of 'green' policies which can be adopted by organisations include:

■ initiatives in the workplace to reduce the consumption of electricity, eg 'turn off the lights and the computers at night' campaigns

■ energy-saving devices such as LED and low-energy lights

■ the use of recycled materials in the office, eg paper and printer toner cartridges

■ using materials from sustainable resources (eg books, such as this one, printed on paper manufactured from forests which are being replanted rather than being depleted)

■ recycling of waste materials, eg paper, plastic, cardboard

■ reducing the 'carbon footprint', eg reducing CO_2 by introducing

  – cycle to work schemes

  – low-emission company cars

  – car sharing schemes

■ requiring suppliers to certify their 'green' credentials, eg farmers supplying supermarkets being required to avoid the use of harmful pesticides

the financial implications of sustainability

The financial implications of sustainability can work in opposite ways on an organisation such as a large business:

■ a sustainability policy can make the business **save money,** but also

■ a sustainability policy can make the business incur **greater costs**

One of the major advantages of cutting down on the use of resources such as energy and paper is that it can **save money**. This means that it can actually pay a business to introduce 'green' policies, for example:

■ a business that runs a fleet of fuel-efficient company cars will have lower fuel costs and receive tax benefits for using low emission vehicles

■ the Government scheme whereby large retailers have to charge customers for plastic bags and give the money received to charitable causes has reduced the number of bags given out and the amount retailers spend on new bags – a saving which also benefits society

Both of these measures benefit the environment and society and cut the running costs of a business.

One of the issues of sustainability is that it sometimes requires businesses **to incur extra costs**, for example:

- ordering packaging made from recycled cardboard and plastics which are more expensive but have been specified by the business to prove its own 'green' credentials

- recycling the packaging used on deliveries from suppliers

- complying with regulations which require modifications to products to ensure that they are environmentally friendly, cars for example

sustainability and social equality

Another important objective of sustainability is the social well-being of people, not just in one locality, but worldwide. At the time of writing there is a distinct lack of equality and well-being. It is estimated, for example, that 1% of the world's population owns a staggering 40% of the world's wealth.

how can sustainability help?

As far as sustainability is concerned 'society' includes a wide range of people and promoting 'social equality' involves many different ways of helping these people. A finance function of a business may get involved in all these areas:

- the **worldwide and national communities**
    - sponsoring events (eg sponsored walks and marathons) to raise funds for charitable causes, eg London Marathon, Comic Relief, Cancer Research UK
    - sponsoring sport and the arts

- the **local community**
    - sponsoring local sports events
    - providing work experience to local school students
    - providing prizes for school and college award ceremonies

- the **organisation** which employs finance staff
    - providing the funds and time off for an employee to take an accounting qualification
    - setting up and funding 'bonding' activities within the department, eg a night out, a white water rafting experience

a high quality product

Another benefit which an organisation can provide for its customers is a high quality of product or service. A product which is environmentally friendly and socially beneficial will help to increase sales and profitability.

CORPORATE SOCIAL RESPONSIBILITY (CSR)

promoting sustainable principles

Businesses such a limited companies and other organisations known to the general public like to promote themselves to their stakeholders and the public in general as being 'green' and socially responsible. This adoption of policies which promote the principles of sustainability is known as **corporate social responsibility**. By 'stakeholders' we mean all the people who have an interest in the business or organisation, for example:

- shareholders who have invested in them if they are public limited companies

- customers who buy from them

- suppliers who supply them

- the local community

- their employees

- the general public

sustainability and Corporate Social Responsibility

The way in which organisations promote a 'green' and socially responsible image is by general advertising and also, in the case of the larger companies by the issue of a **Corporate Social Responsibility (CSR)** document.

The Tesco statement of strategy for sustainable development is set out below.

TESCO

Our seven part strategy sets out clear goals for the business to ensure we deliver long-term sustainable growth. Putting our responsibilities to the communities we serve at the heart of what we do is an essential part of it. By operating responsibly and working with customers, suppliers, expert partners and NGOs our hope is that we can leave the world a better place; a greener, healthier and more prosperous place than when we began.

(Note that a 'NGO' is 'Non-Governmental Organisation').

Corporate Social Responsibility (CSR) initiatives include policies which

■ help to protect the environment

■ help society both locally and worldwide

■ improve the welfare of the workforce

Examples of these are set out below.

protecting the environment

■ installing low consumption electrical devices

■ encouraging staff to save energy by checking that electrical equipment is turned off at the end of the working day

■ reducing CO_2 (carbon dioxide) emissions from premises

■ encouraging staff to use public transport rather than their own cars

■ introducing 'cycle to work' and car sharing schemes

■ recycling of waste material (eg paper, plastic and cardboard)

helping society locally and worldwide

■ sourcing products where possible from renewable resources and where local economies will benefit (eg 'Fair Trade' coffee and bananas)

■ ensuring that the supply chain (eg farmers who supply supermarkets) is also actively supporting sustainable development (environmentally and socially)

■ sponsoring national fund raising events such as the London Marathon

■ sponsoring local sports and arts events

■ setting up links with local schools and colleges

improving the welfare of the workforce

■ providing staff training and promotion prospects

■ providing flexible working so that employees can meet personal commitments (eg picking up from school)

■ offering free gym membership to staff

■ organising social events and 'bonding' events such as activity days out

■ encouraging CPD (Continuing Professional Development), for example providing resources in terms of time and textbooks for professional courses

Chapter Summary

- Ethical behaviour in the workplace involves knowing about and practising basic principles of good and acceptable behaviour.

- Ethical behaviour in the workplace is based on a number of principles, including:
  - honesty and fairness
  - acting in a professional way
  - maintaining confidentiality

- These ethical principles should be observed not only in the workplace, but also out of working hours in situations such as social gatherings.

- The ethical principles of honesty and fairness involve:
  - being truthful, honest and fair
  - avoiding possible conflicts of interest or influencing others to do something that is not ethical

- The ethical principle of acting in a professional way involves:
  - being competent in doing what is expected of you
  - taking care over what you do in the course of your work

- The ethical principle of confidentiality is particularly important because a leak of personal information by an employee could be in breach of the Data Protection Act.

- **Sustainability** is a concept which drives the policies of most organisations.

- The three main objectives of sustainability – also known as the 'three pillars of sustainability are
  - **economic growth**, ie creating profit for the benefit of business owners, employees and the economy in general
  - **environmental protection** – the 'green' factor
  - **social equality** – increasing the well-being of society at large

- Many organisations adopt the policies of sustainability through setting up various initiatives; these are collectively known as 'Corporate Social Responsibility' and contain schemes for:
  - environmental protection
  - helping society locally and worldwide
  - improving the welfare of the workforce

Key Terms

workplace ethics	moral principles and standards which set out how employees should behave when they are at work and representing their employer away from the workplace
honesty and fairness	obeying the rules, being truthful and dealing fairly
confidentiality	knowing when to disclose information held by the organisation and when not to disclose it
professional behaviour	acting in a 'professional' way and not bringing the profession into disrepute
sustainability	policies adopted by people and organisations which are based on the principles of economic growth (profit), environmental protection (planet) and social equality (people)
economic growth	the ways in which the making of profit by a business benefits the business owners, employees and in varying degrees also benefits the local and national economies
environmental protection	policies adopted by organisations which protect and conserve natural resources:
	– energy saving schemes
	– reduction of harmful emissions
	– limiting the use of materials
	– recycling of materials
	– using resources which can be replaced
social equality	policies adopted by organisations which promote the well-being of people both locally and worldwide:
	– charitable giving
	– sponsorship of fund-raising events
	– sponsorship of local arts and sports events
	– supporting schools and colleges
	– supporting employees
Corporate Social Responsibility	the overall strategy of an organisation promoting all areas of sustainability

Activities

8.1 You work in the Accounts Office of a large wholesaler.

Indicate which **one** of the following situations represents a breach of confidentiality.

(a)	You have been asked to send some figures to your company's auditors	
(b)	You email your company's Sales Manager with details of customer credit limits	
(c)	You mention to a member of your family that a shop in the High Street that is one of your customers is having financial problems and is likely to become insolvent	
(d)	One of your customers sends a letter asking you to send sales figures to the bank	

8.2 The three sentences in the table below represent breaches of ethical behaviour.

You are to write in the right-hand column the appropriate ethical principle which is breached in each case. Choose from:

honesty and fairness   **professional behaviour**   **confidentiality**

You mention to your partner that her employer has been refused credit by the company that employs you.	
You 'borrow' £10 from the cash till because you are short of cash for the weekend. You fully intend to put it back on Monday, but you forget as it is such a busy day.	
You hear a colleague at a Friday night pub session in a crowded bar say that his manager is 'useless' and he 'doesn't know how he got his qualifications'.	

8.3 Indicate in the table below which **four** of the following are sustainability policies that a business might adopt.

(a)	A cycle to work scheme	
(b)	A policy of re-using the blank side of A4 white copy paper for printing on	
(c)	Testing the fire extinguishers on a regular basis	
(d)	Putting up a notice telling staff to only fill the kettle with the amount of water needed when making coffee or tea	
(e)	Using company cars which have the most powerful engines	
(f)	Suggesting a team is set up to do a charity walk in support of Cancer Research UK	
(g)	Making sure that everyone has a regular eye test	
(h)	Recommending that the cheapest packaging material is used to save money	

8.4 Indicate which **two** of the following statements is true in relation to sustainability.

(a)	Sustainability involves keeping sales of products at a stable level	
(b)	Computers should be turned off at the end of each working day	
(c)	Sustainability encourages an employer to pay for an employee to train for an accounting qualification	
(d)	It is best to keep lights on at all times because this will mean that the bulbs will last longer	

8.5 You work for a restaurant chain 'Pronta Pizza' as a Management Trainee. Your team has been asked by the Training Manager to investigate various initiatives that could be incorporated into a Corporate Social Responsibility plan for next year. The initiatives must relate to the three principles of sustainability:

- Protecting the environment
- Providing a benefit to the Pronta Pizza employees
- Helping society locally and nationally

The list of initiatives which the team then suggests is shown below:

Suggested initiatives for the Corporate Social Responsibility Plan

(1) Save electricity and gas by not having the ovens on continuously

(2) Divide all tips received between all the employees and ensure that they are not taken by the management

(3) Pay for staff to go on a part-time catering course

(4) Ensure that tips only go to the waiting staff because the kitchen staff do not meet the public

(5) Have 'Please recycle me!' printed on takeaway pizza boxes

(6 Re-use paper napkins which appear to be clean to save on paper wastage

(7) Buy fresh salad and vegetables from local organic suppliers

(8) Display collection boxes for Oxfam in the restaurants

(9) Charge customers £1 extra for take-away pizza boxes

(10) Publicise a 'two for one pizza' special offer for students and senior citizens

---

Tasks

(a) The Training Manager reads through the list and asks you to identify and comment on three suggestions which you think would **not** work as initiatives because they do not comply with the principles of sustainability or with workplace regulations. Set them out in the table below.

(b) You are then asked to sort the remaining listed suggestions into the three sustainability categories and enter them in the table below:

Protecting the environment
Providing a benefit to the Pronta Pizza employees
Helping society locally and nationally

(c) If, as suggested in this scenario, the restaurant management might be taking the tips given to the waiting staff, this would be which of the following (tick the correct answer).

(a)	Contrary to the sustainability principle which protects the environment	
(b)	A breach of the ethical requirement of being honest and trustworthy	
(c)	A breach of the ethical requirement of confidentiality	
(d)	Acceptable practice	

Answers to chapter activities

CHAPTER 1: THE FINANCE FUNCTION – ROLES AND RESPONSIBILITIES

1.1   (d)   It deals with cash, financial records, financial reports, costing and budgets

1.2   (a)   HM Revenue & Customs
        (c)   The company's bank
        (d)   The customers of the business
        (f)   The suppliers of the business

1.3   (a)   Prepares sales and profit reports for senior management

1.4   (c)   Interprets costing data for senior management

1.5   An **internal auditor** is normally an employee of the organisation being audited, but an **external auditor** should be a member of an independent firm of accountants.

1.6   **(a)**   false

        (b)   false

        (c)   true

        (d)   true

1.7   **(a)**   – sales ledger assistant to accounts line manager
                – cashier to accounts line manager
                – payroll assistant to accounts line manager

        (b)   the sales ledger assistant

        (c)   the cashier in the first place, the line manager in the second place

        (d)   purchases ledger, costing, inventory control

CHAPTER 2: EFFECTIVE WORKING IN THE FINANCE FUNCTION

2.1   (a)   Being successful in achieving what you set out to do

2.2   (b)   To complete a job with the minimum of wasted time, effort or expense

2.3   (b)   It must be made within an appropriate timescale
        (c)   It needs to be made using language appropriate to the situation

2.4   (c)   Reply politely with apologies

2.5   (a)   Details of the authorisation needed for business purchases

2.6   (c)   Being able to pay all company debts when they are due

2.7   (b)   Get customers to pay earlier

2.8   (d)   Drawn up by the employer as a guide to employees of health and safety arrangements

CHAPTER 3: FINANCIAL INFORMATION, DOCUMENTATION AND DATA SECURITY

3.1   (b)   The total may not agree with the total on the statement of account sent by the seller

3.2   (a)   The product code may not agree with the description of the goods and so it will need to be queried

3.3   (b)   The amounts sent by the buyer in settlement of invoices must be correctly shown on the statement

3.4   Credit Debit Debit Credit

3.5   Favourable variance: sales are higher than budgeted, costs are lower than budgeted

Adverse variance: sales are lower than budgeted, costs are higher than budgeted

3.6   (c)   Drawing up a cash budget

3.7   (b)   A statement of profit or loss

3.8   (c)   Not releasing personal data to outsiders

3.9   1   pass2A%
       2   G5Thrones
       3   kith33
       4   mypassword

3.10   (a)   At least daily
       (b)   In more than one storage format
       (e)   And stored on the premises and also externally

CHAPTER 4: EFFECTIVE BUSINESS COMMUNICATIONS

4.1   (d)   The message must be clear, correct and on time

4.2   (b) and (c)

4.3   **(a)** They're, **(b)** their, **(c)** There

4.4

Title page

(Executive) Summary

Introduction

Findings (Main Body)

Conclusions

Recommendations

Appendices

4.5

Incorrect word	Correction
239847244	239847224
Mrs	Miss
Colman	Coleman
dissappointed	disappointed
They're	There
faithfully	sincerely

4.6 **(a)** and **(b)**

From	j.mason@frankiesfashionware.co.uk
To	l.wood@frankiesfashionware.co.uk
Subject	Sales data for June **1**

Hi Laura

Please send me the quantity of St Tropez shades (code 9424) **2** sold

during the month of June **3** . We need this information to carry

out a costing exercise. I need the information, please, by 9 July **4** .

Many thanks and kind regards

Jamie

Accounts Department

4.7 **(a)** Missing: name or signature of the person who has written the message, no indication of the percentage discount to be given.

(b) Missing: date, person or department to contact at RF Electronics

4.8 Possible situations might include:

- making an important telephone call which involves complex data

- preparing for a staff appraisal

- preparing a verbal presentation

- attending an important meeting at which you want to bring up a number of different issues

- a 'report back' to colleagues about an internal meeting you have attended

- a 'report back' to colleagues about a meeting with an important customer or supplier

CHAPTER 5: CALCULATIONS AND SPREADSHEETS

5.1

(a)

Product code	Description	Quantity	Price £	Unit	Total £	Discount %	Net £
109BK	Box file (black)	20	4.00	each	80.00	30	56.00
					Total		56.00
					VAT @ 20%		11.20
					TOTAL		67.20

(b)

Product code	Description	Quantity	Price £	Unit	Total £	Discount %	Net £
235RD	Biros (red)	9	5.60	box of ten	50.40	20	40.32
					Total		40.32
					VAT @ 20%		8.06
					TOTAL		48.38

(c)

Product code	Description	Quantity	Price £	Unit	Total £	Discount %	Net £
563BL	Year planners (blue)	8	12.95	each	103.60	10	93.24
					Total		93.24
note that VAT is rounded <u>down</u> to nearest p					VAT @ 20%		18.64
					TOTAL		111.88

5.2   **(a)**   15% discount on an amount of £45.50 = £6.825, rounded to £6.83

(b)   20% discount on an amount of £44.99 = £8.998, rounded to £9.00

(c)   30% discount on an amount of £21.75 = £6.525, rounded to £6.53

(d)   15% discount on an amount of £390.95 = £58.6425, rounded to £58.64

(e)   30% discount on an amount of £964.55 = £289.365, rounded to £289.37

(f)   2.5% discount on an amount of £35.95 = £0.89875, rounded to £0.90

5.3 **(a)** £41.00 + VAT of £8.20

(b) £244.00 + VAT of £48.80

(c) £1.90 + VAT of £0.38

(d) £364.00 + VAT of £72.80

(e) £88.00 + VAT of £17.60

5.4

HYPNOS ENTERPRISES – Annual Sales				
	Forecast £	Actual £	Difference £	Percentage difference
Year 1	600,000	642,000	+ 42,000	7%
Year 2	640,000	608,000	– 32,000	5%

HYPNOS ENTERPRISES – Annual Profits				
	Forecast £	Actual £	Difference £	Percentage difference
Year 1	64,000	67,200	+ 3,200	5%
Year 2	65,000	63,050	– 1,950	3%

Comments could include the fact that both sales and profits were better than expected in Year 1, but worse than forecast in Year 2. Decisions will have to be made by management.

It could be mentioned that action is likely to have to be taken to stop the drop in sales and profits.

Students should not be expected to go further than this and should appreciate that it is the role of management to take the necessary decisions

5.5 • mean £9.33

• median £7.90

• mode £11.00

The mean is the most arithmetically reliable as it takes all values into consideration.

CHAPTER 6: PLANNING AND MANAGING YOUR WORK

6.1 (c) Carry on with your own work until you have the opportunity to refer the problem to your line
           manager when she is free

6.2

Your line manager asks you for the balances of your top 20 customer accounts. She needs the information for a meeting that morning.	**urgent**
Your line manager asks you to provide information from the office for the accountants who are coming in next week to audit the accounts. You have never done this before as this is normally a senior colleague's responsibility.	**one-off 'ad hoc'**
Your colleague reminds you that it is your turn to get the milk from Tesco Express and remarks that the milk has run out.	**non-urgent**

6.3

Category of task	Reason
urgent and important	if you don't do this task soon you are going to let a lot of people down
urgent but less important	your manager asks you to turn down the heating
important but not urgent	setting up a spreadsheet for a meeting in a week's time
neither important nor urgent	sending round a suggestion list for a staff social

6.4

An employee's personal record of tasks and events over a long period of time.	**diary**
A detailed plan which involves a number of people and interrelated tasks and events for a specific purpose over a period of time.	**action plan**
An annual guide which can be used to display staff holidays and external training courses.	**wall planner**
An employee's daily personal record of tasks to be done in the short term.	**'to do' list**

Task 6.5

(a)

WEDNESDAY/THURSDAY/FRIDAY 'TO DO' LIST (in order of completion)	
Task 1	Process the payroll (BACS and cash)
Task 2	Update and balance the petty cash book
Task 3	Visit the bank to pick up cash wages and petty cash top up
Task 4	Lock the cash in the safe at work
Task 5	Make up cash pay packets and distribute payslips for all employees

(b)

	Serious	Not serious
The staff may not get paid on time	✔	
The cash from the bank may not get locked away	✔	
Petty cash reimbursements may be delayed		✔
Suppliers may not get paid on time	✔	
Minor office duties may not get done		✔

CHAPTER 7: DEVELOPING PERSONAL SKILLS IN THE WORKPLACE

7.1

Situation	Interpersonal skill
(a) Admiring a colleague who is able to process sales invoices quickly and accurately	respecting others
(b) Learning that a particular colleague will give the correct answer to a question	developing trust
(c) A colleague who will always get a task done on time and with no mistakes	being reliable
(d) A colleague who gives you instructions which you can easily follow	communicating effectively
(e) A colleague who always dresses smartly and deals with customers politely	presenting a professional image
(f) A colleague who is in charge of the computer input staff and answerable for what they do	being responsible

7.2   (c)   Using the skills and having the knowledge expected of their occupation

7.3   (c)   Welcoming and shaking hands with the customer

7.4   (b)   Members understand their role in the team and what they have to do
        (c)   Members are prepared to carry out tasks for other members if necessary
        (e)   Members must maintain good levels of communication with each other

7.5   (c)   It would reflect badly on the Department and also the business because suppliers may not get paid on time and errors occur

7.6   (b)   Mention the problem to your line manager if the situation does not improve

7.7   **Stages**   **Statements**

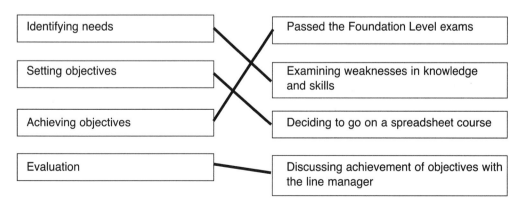

CHAPTER 8: ETHICS, SUSTAINABILITY AND CORPORATE SOCIAL RESPONSIBILITY

8.1 (c) You mention to a member of your family that a shop in the High Street that is one of your customers is having financial problems and is likely to become insolvent

8.2

You mention to your partner that her employer has been refused credit by the company that employs you.	**confidentiality**
You 'borrow' £10 from the cash till because you are short of cash for the weekend. You fully intend to put it back on Monday, but you forget as it is such a busy day.	**honesty and fairness**
You hear a colleague at a Friday night pub session in a crowded bar say that his manager is 'useless' and he 'doesn't know how he got his qualifications'.	**professional behaviour**

8.3 (a) A cycle to work scheme

   (b) A policy of re-using the blank side of A4 white copy paper for printing on

   (d) Putting up a notice telling staff to only fill the kettle with the amount of water needed when making coffee or tea

   (f) Suggesting a team is set up to do a charity walk in support of Cancer Research UK

8.4 (b) Computers should be turned off at the end of each working day

   (c) Sustainability encourages an employer to pay for an employee to train for an accounting qualification

8.5 (a) (4) Ensure that tips only go to the waiting staff because the kitchen staff do not meet the public.
      (Comment: this would be very unfair on the kitchen staff)

   (6) Re-use paper napkins which appear to be clean to save on paper wastage.
      (Comment: this would be very unhygienic and contrary to health and safety principles)

   (9) Charge customers £1 extra for take-away pizza boxes.
      (Comment: this would be unpopular with customers as they are used to having free boxes. The suggestion for 'Please recycle me!' printed on the box would be far more effective.

(b) **Protecting the environment**

        (1)   Save electricity and gas by not having the ovens on continuously.

        (5)   Have 'Please recycle me!' printed on takeaway pizza boxes

        (7)   Buy fresh salad and vegetables from local organic suppliers

Providing a benefit to the Pronta Pizza employees

        (2)   Divide all tips received between all the employees and ensure that they are not taken by the management

        (3)   Pay for staff to go on a part-time catering course

Helping society locally and nationally

        (8)   Display collection boxes for Oxfam in the restaurants

        (10)   Publicise a 'two for one pizza' special offer for students and senior citizens

(c)   (b)   A breach of the ethical requirement of being honest and trustworthy

Index

for your notes

for your notes

for your notes

for your notes

for your notes